LIVING ON TARGET

A Lifestyle of Discipleship

KELVIN SMITH

LIVING ON TARGET

Copyright © 2009, 2011 by Kelvin Smith

ISBN: 978-0-9793192-4-2

Published by

LIFEBRIDGE
BOOKS
P.O. BOX 49428
CHARLOTTE, NC 28277

Printed in the United States of America.

CONTENTS

PREFACE

We were driving home from Atlanta to Charlotte. Our car held four quiet and frustrated pastors who had been attending a ministry conference.

As the lead pastor of our church, I had been deeply moved by the Holy Spirit to focus on discipleship. The Great Commission: *"...and make disciples of all nations,"* echoed in my ears. These were my Lord's last words before He ascended to His Father. This was His final command before sending the Holy Spirit to indwell His followers. This commission reflected *His* heart— and the call to obey Him was burning in *mine.* I wanted desperately to shepherd His Body so that they would be well pleasing to Him. His call to discipleship could not be ignored.

Each pastor on our team shared the vision. We had registered for this conference on "Small Groups and Discipleship" with hope and readiness. We were primed! We knew that discipleship was an imperative for the furthering of the Kingdom. We anticipated returning home with direction and focus. Instead, here we were, driving in silence, conscious only of a deep disappointment.

Jesus had called us to *be* and to *make* disciples. That was the "What." No one at the conference had even begun to address the "How," and this is what we were becoming more and more determined to discover.

Like a summer rain, starting with a few drops and building into a downpour, the conversation in the car became a deluge of questions:

- What *is* biblical discipleship?
- How many disciples have we trained lately?
- What does a *mature* disciple look like?
- What are the major issues surrounding discipleship in our church—in our culture?
- How does real discipleship impact our personal lives, our marriages, our parenting and our finances?
- Are there any consistently effective ways to *implement* the discipling process?

WHY, WHAT, WHO, AND HOW

Over the next few years, the Lord began to show us the answers to these basic, yet essential questions. Discipleship is a lifestyle. Discipleship is a process.

"Living On Target" explains *why* we are called to such lives, *what* discipleship looks like, *who* empowers the process, and *how* it is to be carried out in practice.

Many of us have read books that exhort the church to make disciples, yet they often seem to lack the instructions. This book is our humble attempt to answer some of the questions in the discipling process.

Beyond theory, what you are about to discover has been implemented and practiced for years and is being found to bear much fruit. We certainly do not claim perfection in this endeavor, but our goal is to be faithful. We invite you into this learning process with us.

Living on Target is a lifestyle that the Lord developed naturally as we identified four core foundations that generally encompass all the areas of our lives. Then we identified the spiritual disciplines within those foundations that, if practiced under the control of the Holy Spirit, would yield a mature and reproductive life in Christ. This gave us an effective framework to use in clarifying our own walk as disciples and gave us a dynamic lifestyle to use in biblically discipling others.

I believe you picked up this book for a reason. Wherever you are on your journey, may God take you deeper with Him. May you be challenged and blessed to know that He not only calls you to be well pleasing to Him, but He gives you the power to obey Him—and enjoy Living on Target for Him.

THE IMPACT

Since our church has been transformed by this message, we have received countless testimonies of how it has impacted lives. Here are just a few:

———————➤———————

In a world that competes for our attention daily, Living on Target provides a Christ centered approach to make sure we stay on God's path of life, and not the world's. It was the beginning of the life-changing work God wanted for me. It never grows old and is never finished.

I went through the Living on Target discipling process and it has indeed made a remarkable difference in my life. Not only did I realize even more significantly, the importance of my intimate relationship with Christ, but the extent to which every aspect of life is impacted by this relationship.

As a male, I sometimes identify myself with my occupation. I've now learned that my true occupation is Living on Target, and what I do for money is simply a part of that. It also helps when things/life get out of control. Now I know where to go first, then second, etc., to get back on the track God has planned.

Living on Target is filled with practical ways to recognize and to demonstrate the truths of God's Word, not only in each believer's life but to also disciple and impact the lives of other Christians. This is essential as we prepare to one day stand before a holy God and give a good account.

I have both attended and led a Living on Target group. The benefits and the relationships that are built have lasted well beyond the time spent in the meetings. The focus of living as the Word teaches us about our spouses, family, church and community has been a blessing and something every believer should take time to invest in.

———————▶———————

Using Living on Target as a discipling process is a beautiful way to live out the profound principles of Scripture. I have seen this radical change in myself and in countless others whom I have discipled.

———————▶———————

I have grown tremendously as I have led several Target groups. This has greatly improved my ability to share my own trials and victories in a transparent way, and to encourage others to become disciplers themselves.

INTRODUCTION

Therefore, we make it our aim, whether
present or absent, to be well pleasing to Him.
– 2 CORINTHIANS 5:9

Living on Target is intended for everyone.

This book is written with tremendous love and passion for Christ, His church, and for those who are not yet believers. The message is simple, yet when it is truly understood and practiced from the heart, its truth will transform every person into God's likeness and bring Him much pleasure.

Many say they believe in Jesus Christ as their Lord and Savior, yet their lifestyles do not reflect this. They may know *about* God, but how many truly *know* Him? They take aim at the temporal, empty distractions of life, but the Lord has called us to focus on a vital, faithful, contagious, consistently growing relationship with Him—one that naturally causes us to live out what we believe. We must abandon cultural Christianity and embrace biblical Christianity.

God has not only *called* us, but He has *given His clear directions* for adjusting our aim so that we can know and please Him, and model true Christianity before the world! His call and His empowerment allow us to center on becoming disciples who are growing, maturing, sharing, and that are transparent.

I, and every leader of Christ's Church, will give an account to God for what we teach (James 3:1) and how we watch over the souls He has entrusted to us (Hebrews 13:17). With this understanding, I submit this book unto Him and you with great humility and godly fear.

Even though I have prayed repeatedly that God would inspire this book through me, I fully realize my humanity. I encourage you to search the Scriptures daily to see if these things are so (Acts 17:11).

I truly believe this book will be very fruitful because it is saturated with the Word of God and we know that His Word (not mine) will never come back void. I pray that it convicts, encourages, affirms, and drives us to be and to make disciples for His glory…while we wait for His return.

I echo the apostle Paul in Colossians 1:28: *"Him we preach, warning every man and teaching every man in all wisdom, that we may present every man [every person] perfect [or mature] in Christ Jesus."*

The process of *being* and *making* disciples allows us to walk in truth and to share it with others, developing a biblical world view, as well as a biblical view of the church. Living on Target serves as a starting point for every believer, fully realizing the need for additional doctrinal study.

A devoted disciple will adjust his lifestyle to make sure he is joyfully and fervently *Living on Target* today—so that on the day he gives an account of his life before God, he will hear those precious words. "Well done, My good and faithful servant. Enter into the joy of your Lord."

— *Kelvin Smith*

ONE

WHAT ARE YOU AIMING FOR?

Therefore I do not run like a man running aimlessly;
I do not fight like a man beating the air.
– 1 CORINTHIANS 9:26 (NIV)

The Apostle Paul, the great missionary for Christ, did not run his race of faith *aimlessly*. He was very disciplined, desiring to labor for our Lord in a manner that would bring Him glory. That should be our aim as well!

You have probably heard the saying, "If you aim at nothing, you are sure to hit it." The same principle is true in our spiritual life. If we aim at nothing, we can be certain we will achieve nothing of eternal value.

Most of us are aiming for something. Sad to say, much of what we are targeting pertains only to *this* world and *this* life—because our world revolves exclusively around us and for us. We usually have happiness as our objective, which we equate with finding the human love of our life, entertainment, money, houses, cars, traveling, eating, and drinking.

None of these, in and of themselves, are wrong or evil, but when they become our primary *aim*, these goals will certainly leave us empty and wanting more:

- Without question, our *flesh* tells us to serve ourselves.
- Our *enemy*, Satan, certainly tempts us to attend only to our self-interests.
- Our *culture* undoubtedly entices us with a "me first" philosophy.

This characteristic of selfishness will be very prevalent as we approach the return of our Lord. Jesus declared, *"And <u>as it was in the days of Noah,</u> so it will be also in the days of the Son of Man: They ate, they drank, they married wives, they were given in marriage, until the day that Noah entered the ark, and the flood came and destroyed them all. <u>Likewise as it was also in the days of Lot</u>: They ate, they drank, they bought, they sold, they planted, they built...<u>Even so will it be in the day when the Son of Man is revealed</u>"* (Luke 17:26-28,30. Also see Matthew 24: 36-39). Does this sound like our society today?

Now again, there's nothing wrong with working hard, living life, and celebrating life's events, but when these become the primary goal of a person's life in totality without any regard for Christ, His coming, His Kingdom, or His mission, then we are completely missing the mark, and we'll give an account for it when He returns.

Paul addressed this in Philippians 3 where he listed all the achievements he had accomplished in the flesh. He stated in verse 8 that he counted all things loss for the excellence of the knowledge of Jesus His Lord—considering them as rubbish that he might gain Christ. He invited his brothers and sisters in the faith to join him in following his example and he warned them against modeling their lives after those who set their minds on earthly things.

In Philippians 3:17- 4:1, Paul stated, *"Brethren, join in following my example, and note those who so walk, as you have us for a pattern. For many walk, of whom I have told you often, and now tell you even weeping, that they are the enemies of the cross of Christ: whose end is destruction, whose god is their belly, and whose glory is in their shame—who set their mind on earthly things. For our citizenship is in heaven from which we also eagerly wait for the Savior, the Lord Jesus Christ who will transform our lowly body that it may be conformed to His glorious body according to the working by which He is even able to subdue all things unto Himself. Therefore, my beloved and longed-for brethren, my joy and crown, so stand fast in the Lord, beloved."*

He is reminding us to stand fast in Christ as we aim, not for earthly objectives, but for *spiritual* goals.

WHAT ABOUT TOMORROW?

Have we lost a sense of the eternal? Consider the words of Randy Alcorn in his book *The Law of Rewards:*

A startling thing has happened among Western

Christians. Many of us habitually think and act as if there were no eternity—or as if what we do in this present life has no eternal consequences...

The trend is to focus on our present circumstances instead of our eternal future. Yet Scripture states that eternal realities should influence the character of our present life, right down to every word we speak and every action we take (James 2:12; 2 Peter 3:11-12)...

Our brief stay here may appear unimportant, but nothing could be further from the truth. The Bible tells us that although others may not remember us or care what our lives here have been, God will remember perfectly, and he cares very much—so much that the door of eternity swings on the hinges of our present lives.

The Bible tells us that this life lays the foundation upon which eternal life is built. _Eternity will hold for us what we have invested there during our life on earth._

Scripture makes clear that the one central business of this life is to prepare for the next.

Romans 2:6-8 states that God _"will render to each one according to his deeds: eternal life to those who by patient continuance in doing good seek for glory, honor, and immortality; but to those who are self-seeking and do not obey the truth, but obey unrighteousness—indignation and wrath"_.

Our finite minds cannot comprehend the longevity of eternity. Eternal life is just that—eternal—never ending. Our life on earth is very short and what is accomplished in and for Christ will last for eternity.

I am sure we can all agree that time doesn't stand still for anyone. Our birthdays seem to come quicker every year. Time on this earth in its present state is short. *"...For what is your life? It is even a vapor that appears for a little time and then vanishes away."* (James 4:14) Eternity is forever ...prepare for it!

There is nothing more important than loving and glorifying God as we live by faith in an intimate and obedient relationship with Him. Biblical faith will be demonstrated by our trust in God and our obedience to His Word. The Bible tells us that it is impossible to please God without faith (Hebrews 11:6). We please Him when our faith is active.

Salvation through faith in Christ alone is absolutely free, yet our faith in Him will be proven genuine only as we trust and obey Him (James 2:18). Faithful people establish their spiritual life as their top priority.

Jesus taught us about spiritual priorities when He instructed us to, *"seek first the kingdom of God and His righteousness..."* (Matthew 6:33). Establishing and maintaining a biblical spiritual target equips us to aim for eternity and grow as we progress on our journey.

Paul had such a target. He said, *"Therefore we make it our aim, whether present or absent, to be well pleasing to Him"* (2 Corinthians 5:9). The word "aim" can be defined as "ambition," "goal," or "the ability to hit a target." We should absolutely make our spiritual goals a high priority and they should be the filter through which we live life.

17

God knows every detail of our lives. He knows our victories and challenges, our dreams and our hurts. He also knows our priorities. So, what are we aiming for? Is it all about us, or is it for the glory of God and His kingdom?

In order to be well pleasing to the Lord, I submit that the following four foundations should be targeted to become vital parts of our lifestyle, both personally and corporately as a church.

The Four Foundations are:

1. **Living in Love and Service to Christ**
    Becoming men and women of *prayer*, the *Word*, and *personal worship*.

2. **Living in Love and Service in the Home**
    Placing our homes, singleness, marriages, children and finances in biblical order.

3. **Living in Love and Service to the Church**
    Loving the Bride of Christ and being united in purpose. Ministering to the poor, the persecuted and those in need.

4. **Living in Love and Service to the World**
    Loving and pursuing the lost. Evangelizing and discipling. Giving a clear, authentic witness for Christ and His salvation.

Please notice that the word "living" in each foundation is in the present tense. This target is not a temporary program or just an academic Bible study. It is, indeed, a *lifestyle*.

These four foundations need to be integral anchors for our lives. They are simple, biblical cornerstones, yet very profound. If the Church were to operate faithfully in these four areas as a lifestyle, it would drastically transform us, impact our relationships, and change the world!

THE CHURCH THAT "COULD BE"

Dream with me for a moment of a church where everyone is living faithfully (not perfectly, but *faithfully*) and lovingly in these four foundational areas. Can you envision a church where everyone experiences intimacy with Christ on a daily basis, where our homes are in biblical order, where we bask in joyful marriages, train up godly and faithful children, exert disciplined control over God's money, and where we properly deal with materialism in our daily walk?

Imagine a church that is characterized by their genuine love for one another. See a community where all of the members participate in the mission Christ has given us to accomplish! Dream of a church where we love the lost and remember the poor; where we evangelize and then disciple those who are saved; and where we are united in purpose.

This is exactly what Christ has called us to. It is definitely possible as we depend on the Holy Spirit and keep our eyes fixed on the heavenly goal. We may not be perfect in these areas, but we can and should be faithful. This discipling process is a lifestyle and we will never finish it until God takes us to our eternal home.

The harvest is indeed ripe—yet the workers are still few. Why? I believe it is a heart and order issue. Many of us, sad to say, are out of order in one or more of these foundations —especially the first two. If our personal relationship with

Christ and our family is not in order and intimate, then we find our hearts wavering and even becoming impotent in serving the church or the world. This must change!

Many of us are spinning plates of busyness, chaos, apathy and disorder, which causes us to be ineffective in our witness for Christ.

Satan is the author of confusion, yet we know God is the God of order. Jesus came to earth as a Man, died on a cross, and rose again to bring us life in all of its richness and fullness. We have to receive and practice *Him* as a lifestyle in order to experience His presence. Submitting to God and His biblical order brings forth His peace, freedom, and power...which is available to us all. Don't retreat! Press into God and His Word!

A Strategy with an Objective

We have available to us many tremendous Bible teachers, ministry programs, messages on CDs and DVDs, and we should be thankful for these resources. At the same time, we must be careful not to run from Bible study to Bible study without honestly evaluating these four critical areas in our lives. Paul said, *"Examine yourselves as to whether you are in the faith. Test yourselves..."* (2 Corinthians 13:5). Don't be afraid of truthful self-examination. It truly is for our benefit. It keeps us humble and keeps us from living hypocritical lives.

If we're not careful, we can fall into the same trap the Pharisees did. They understood the Law of God extremely well, yet only in their head; the Scriptures had not gripped their hearts. As a matter of fact, in the Gospels Jesus addressed the Pharisees as hypocrites. He said that they honored God with their lips but their heart was far from Him (Mark 7:7).

Hypocrisy is intentionally giving people the impression that you are living one way when, in fact, you are not. Being faithful means that through the power of God within you, your desire and habit is to obey Him. Faithfulness is evidenced by a pattern of the heart and actions...consistently moving in the direction of maturity, deepening fellowship with God and service to Him and to people.

If our hearts are not drawn into relationship with God and people, our academic Bible knowledge only confirms our hypocrisy. It is very important to know and understand theology, but...**remember, the Sacred Scriptures should always move our hearts toward Him and others.**

Many of us are tempted to tell the world what the Bible teaches...yet we don't live it ourselves. We are much more effective if we first put our heart, life and house in biblical order before we "talk Bible" with others.

An example of this is a brother who delights in being dogmatic about non-essential doctrinal issues. He loves to debate others about doctrine, while at the very same time he continuously mistreats his wife and his children. Yet he refuses to see his sin and repent. (Hypocrite!)

The Word of God must penetrate deep into our hearts and minds. It must then flow out of us to influence people through relationships, which is something we seem to be struggling with today. It is an objective that God absolutely wants us to achieve because the Almighty is all about relationships —first of all with us, and then, as we develop our fellowship with Him, He desires to see this duplicated within our homes, with our spouses, our children, our extended family, and throughout the world.

The Lord longs for us to have our finances under control and materialism in check so that we will indeed have the integrity, passion, and desire to love and serve the Church, to disciple Her and then to also have the time, availability and heartfelt concern to pursue and serve the lost.

As the unsaved receive Christ, we need to be able to train them in the same manner we have been taught. *The divine art of discipleship needs to be rediscovered by believers in the Church today. Living on Target is a strategy to achieve this objective.*

THE NEED FOR BALANCE

Until we have our own lives in biblical order we will be unable to disciple others effectively. Our Christian walk is not just so we can prepare for the day we stand before God, but so we can also live a fruitful, joyful, and purposeful life while we're here on this earth.

These four foundations simply cannot be violated. If they are—although we may be doing *good* things, we are certainly not going to accomplish the eternally *best* things.

To be well pleasing to our heavenly Father, we need to be living in faithful balance in all four of these foundations. Certainly we all have room to grow toward maturity in the Lord, but if we don't make them our priority then we will never see them achieved.

In the church we tend to lean toward extremes or focus in on things that we personally value. For example, we hear of people who claim to love Christ, but don't have a love for the Church, His Bride. How can this be?

Certainly I fully understand the disappointments, unmet

expectations, and even disagreements and hurts in the Church, but if you make the statement, "I love *Jesus*, but I don't love the *Church*," then there is a disconnect.

This inconsistency shows itself in a variety of ways. Some may enjoy attending church services, but they haven't surrendered to Christ. Others serve the church, but not their families.

We've heard too many stories where pastors or Christian leaders (even passionate believers) love everybody else, but their families see their hypocritical activities and feel very unloved. Some may love and serve the lost, but they don't love the Church. Others may love Christ and their families, but they turn their backs on the unsaved. Sometimes believers fear that those who are unsaved may have a negative effect on them or their family.

We must remember that we were all lost at one time and we needed love from God and His church. To become well developed and fully devoted followers of Christ we must mature in love and service in all four of these foundations.

THE RESULTS OF WRONG PRIORITIES

A pastor friend shared with me that at one time he had lost his love for the Church. His ministry to the Body of Christ had begun with a desire to be a godly pastor. But having been hurt by those who had taught him in the Scriptures, he did not see authenticity modeled...nor was there room for transparency or care to be extended *to* as well as *from* the pastor. As he told me, "I had not yet learned that you must humble yourself to be cared for by the Body before you can care for Her."

"After forty-one years, my love for the Church had departed—and *yet I was still serving Her.*" It was an unhealthy, destructive alliance...an error for which his wife and family were also paying a price.

My friend became convicted and distressed, challenged with the fact he was serving the church at the expense of his family. Late at night, when his loved ones were asleep, the phone would ring. A member of the congregation needed his counsel and attention. His wife began chiding, "Your other woman is calling." (My friend's face reflected the depth of impact which this had on him.) His children were asking for him, wishing he "wasn't at the church all the time."

He knew he couldn't continue. Something was terribly wrong. He left the church and determined not to re-engage.

Several years later, the Lord led him to our fellowship and the Living on Target message and lifestyle. Even though he had pastored and served congregations, he humbled himself and began to allow himself to be discipled.

He told me, "As I learned the truths presented in Living on Target, I discovered with great clarity and conviction that before I could passionately and healthfully love and serve the church and the world, I had to focus first and foremost on my relationship with Christ. He was to be my first love. Having my home in order meant that my wife was to feel my preference and protection. She and our children were my ministry—in fact 'ministry' was not reserved for the church. I was called to serve my Lord first, then my family, then the church and then the world. I had it backwards."

He continued, "I am in love with the Church again! She now reminds me how to love and serve my God and my family as well as the Church and beyond. The Body of Christ is no longer functioning as a mistress, but as a sweet reminder that I am part of Her and that God has called us to love our Bridegroom together. I can still slip into the traps of the early years. But I am responsible now to the Holy Spirit's correction and precious people who remind me of God's truth. Psalm 40 anchors me: *'Behold, I come... My ears You have opened... I delight to do Your will, O my God.'"*

AN OVERVIEW

An unbalanced and aimless Christian life will lead to a fruitless and sorrow-filled existence. Many of us have experienced the consequences of this already...or maybe even now are experiencing them. Please know that there is forgiveness, healing, and renewed hope available through God and His Word!

The reason for this teaching based on God's Word, is that there is a remedy for aimless living. There is clear hope and direction for avoiding the consequences of a fruitless life. We must grow and mature in all four of the foundational areas we have been discussing in order for us to *get*—and *stay* spiritually healthy and balanced.

Let me give you a brief overview of the four foundations within The Target, which need to be lived out in the specific order below. Later we will study them in detail.

1. Living In Love and Service to Christ

This is certainly *the* most crucial of all the four. It is our vertical relationship. Without this relationship to our Lord, we cannot live fruitful lives in the other three areas. The Christian walk was not intended to be a journey in the flesh. Christ must live His life in and through us!

We must truly aim for this essential foundation on a daily basis. When we arise each morning, we need to have this objective written on our hearts. To become a man or woman of *prayer, the Word* and *personal worship* is imperative. These spiritual disciplines lead and allow us to have a marvelous relationship with God and they are to be practiced continually. <u>Before we can disciple others in their relational walk with God, we must first be faithful in ours</u>.

If we violate this foundation, the rest of what we do will simply be religious activity. We need to become absolutely grounded in love and intimacy with our Lord. *Then,* we have the privilege of discipling others as to how they too can achieve this special intimacy with Him.

2. Living in Love and Service in the Home

As we live in relationship with God, the first people who should be experiencing the overflow of our closeness with the Lord are those who live with us. <u>Our vertical relationship with Him should positively affect every horizontal relationship on earth, beginning with our families</u>. We are to put our *homes, singleness, marriages, our children, and finances* in order, so that love, acceptance, and peace are being experienced by others through us. Many of us are so challenged in our homes, with our singleness, with our marriages, raising our children, dealing with money, materialism, entertainment, and other activities of life...that there is nothing left in us to love and serve the Church and the world.

If we are living under the control of the Holy Spirit in love and service within our homes, we will be positioned well to serve the Church and disciple others in these areas.

3. Living in Love and Service to the Church

When we become faithful in living out the first two foundations, it positions us to function in love and service without being two-faced. Now we are able to operate as role models and disciplers, fulfilling our purpose together to serve in a manner that would bring honor and glory to His name—to love and serve the poor, the persecuted and the Church for whom Jesus died.

4. Living in Love and Service to the World

Scripture teaches us that we are not *of* the world, but we live *in* the world. We are all here for a divine purpose, part of which is to evangelize our neighbors and the nations to bring them to Christ—not only to know Him but also to make Him known.

When we have these foundations in their proper order and priority—Christ, Home, Church, and the World—something dynamic takes place. As we meet, love and develop relationships with those who are lost, we will be a powerful witness to them. When an unbeliever crosses the line of faith and begins his or her journey as a disciple, we then have a lifestyle of faithfulness and obedience to emulate for them. This is why the Apostle Paul could say, *"Imitate me, just as I also imitate Christ"* (1 Corinthians 11:1).

This gives us the privilege to ask the new disciple, "Would you allow me to:"

- Teach and model for you how to live in relationship with the Lord?

- Teach and model for you how to become a man or woman of prayer, the Word and worship?
- Teach and model for you how to put your home in biblical order with your singleness, your marriage, your children, and your money?
- Teach and model for you how to love and serve the church and the world? Then, just as I began a relationship with you, you will also go and do the same with someone else.

When a person becomes a Christian or when we lead a man, woman, or child to Christ, we should be able to model for them what someone else has modeled for us. Can you dream of a church that will function like this? It is possible! <u>Living on Target would help in the process of reestablishing discipleship in the Church.</u>

If you have not been previously discipled, then please consider, after reading and beginning to practice the Living on Target material...passing this on to others. Paul charges Timothy, *"And the things that you have heard from me among many witnesses, <u>commit these to faithful men who will be able to teach others also</u>"* (2 Timothy 2:2). By discipling others you will be fulfilling our Lord's command to, *"Go therefore and make disciples of all the nations, baptizing them in the name of the Father and of the Son and of the Holy Spirit, teaching them to observe all things that I have commanded you; and lo, I am with you always, even to the end of the age"* (Matthew 28:19-20). This is our mandate! This is how He has called us to advance His kingdom

—through evangelism and discipleship. Glory to God! His Kingdom advances!

IT IS POWERFUL!

As one of our members expressed:

Living on Target has a beautiful way of making simple truths profoundly affect our lives. I have seen this radical change in both myself and countless others with whom I have gone through this teaching and discipling process.

One of the aspects I value most about the Target group is the ability it has to create a sense of community. In the weeks you spend together you share intimately about yourself and learn much regarding each other. It establishes a deep and safe environment in which to share and be held accountable. I truly learned to rejoice with those who rejoice and grieve with those who grieve and in it we became united, the Body of Christ.

From personal experience and from the testimonies of those who have been discipled through this process, I can tell you without hesitation, *"it is powerful!"*

As we evangelize people and disciple believers, it is important to remember that we can live faithfully and obey as wholeheartedly as possible. Even so, God has called us to what can sometimes be a messy task!

Some will not listen to the Lord's call to discipleship. Some will rebel for a time and then repent and be drawn back into fellowship. We can faithfully pray and work and rest in His sovereign power to change our lives first...and then to work in those we are privileged to disciple.

Never give up on people...though you may need to release them from your discipling relationship for a while...or even indefinitely. Someone else may be better suited for them at the time. Always leave the door open...allowing the person to re-approach you in the future. Remember, people are not projects. They are human beings made in the image of God, created to have fellowship with Him. Don't force, control, or manipulate. Love and pray for them.

We can never make people stay in relationship with us or be discipled by us. God sovereignly brings discipling relationships together. We can only make ourselves available to others and we must leave the "heart surgery" to God. Allow the Holy Spirit to accomplish His work and may we stay faithful to ours.

IT'S A LIFESTYLE!

The word "discipleship" or the phrase "go and make disciples" has been quite daunting to some people. They feel fearful or incapable of discipling others.

Our enemy wants us to believe this lie, but rest assured, it is not true. As the Holy Spirit empowers us to live faithfully in these four foundations and practice them as a lifestyle, we can all turn to someone who enters the faith (your spouse, child, friend, neighbor, co-worker, etc.) and <u>simply model</u> for them how we are to be living. Don't let this intimidate you. People will be drawn to your honest faithfulness—struggles and all!

Paul was not perfect in his flesh, nor will you or I ever be. This is why we are instructed in the Bible not to walk in our flesh, but by the Spirit of God. The Lord's provisions are perfect and complete. We have this promise: *"His divine power has given to us all things that pertain to life and godliness, through the knowledge of Him who called us by glory and virtue"* (2 Peter 1:3).

We have everything we need in His divine nature to Live on Target for His glory. Yet, we must continually partake of His divine nature within us in order to live a fruitful and godly life.

This should excite and exhilarate us as Christians—that we have the privilege of being His disciple and discipling others in the faith and that God has provided us with all the resources.

This process must be intentional. We must eliminate anything that would hinder us from <u>being</u> and <u>making</u> disciples. Living on Target is not a temporary program, it is a permanent lifestyle which will bring pleasure to God. Is this your aim?

REFLECT AND RESPOND

- What specific spiritual goals have you been aiming for?

- In what areas have your earthly goals seemed to take preference over your spiritual goals?

- Do you believe that a specific spiritual target will help you on your spiritual journey? In what way?

- Do you believe that these four foundations need to be put in order for you to be a fruitful disciple of Christ?

    1. Living in Love and Service to Christ
    2. Living in Love and Service in the Home
    3. Living in Love and Service to the Church
    4. Living in Love and Service to the World

- What foundational area(s) do you need to address and mature in?

Remember, with God nothing is impossible!

Two

OUR APPOINTMENT WITH GOD

*Therefore we make it our aim, whether
present or absent, to be well pleasing to Him.
For we must all appear before the judgment seat of
Christ, that each one may receive the things done
in the body, according to what he has done,
whether good or bad. Knowing, therefore, the
terror (or fear) of the Lord, we persuade men.*
– 2 CORINTHIANS 5:9-11

Ready or not, an appointment with God is coming for every person. Unbelievers will be judged for their rejection of Christ. Believers and unbelievers will be judged for their works (Revelation 20:13-15, 1 Corinthians 3:11-15).

The Apostle Paul gave his life to persuade people to reconcile to God and prepare to meet Him face to face. He knew that the character of God included love, grace and holiness. That is why he so deeply feared (or revered) Him. I am very concerned that many of us in the Body of Christ have lost, or even never had, a true understanding of the character of God.

REDEFINING GOD?

Unfortunately, many people are making up a god in their minds that simply does not exist. It seems that God has been reduced to an optional choice to follow, a genie to go to when we sense a felt need, or someone to blame or curse when things don't go our way. He is none of these! He is the Lord God Almighty. He has always been and will always be—Holy!

No one has the authority to redefine God or His character. We are not to determine for ourselves who He is or how to have a relationship with Him. He is not interested in people's opinions or their "new" definitions or ideas about Him. His Word tells us who He is and how to have a relationship with Him.

We are to submit to Him and His Word (not our word or opinion—but His Word). *Getting to heaven is determined by who we believe and place our faith in (Christ alone). What we experience at our appointment with God...and in eternity will be determined by how we live out our faith on earth.*

Are you ready for your appointment with God? Let us all stay alert and prepare ourselves for His return. "*...now it is high time to awake out of sleep; for now our salvation is nearer than when we first believed*" (Romans 13:11).

How do we prepare to meet Him? As we abide in Christ

and the power of the Holy Spirit, we will be enabled to live a life of love, grace, and holiness in godly fear. These are characteristics of God that should flow from every Christian's heart as we aim to be well pleasing to our Lord and anticipate our appointment with Him. These three characteristics should be the motivation and foundational reasons for Living on Target. Let's look at each of these characteristics in more detail.

1. LOVE

God *is* love and His love is steadfast (1 John 4:8 and Psalm 145:8-9).

The Bible is abundantly clear regarding the fact that God loves you. We read in John 3:16, *"For God so loved the world that He gave His only begotten Son, that whoever believes in Him should not perish but have everlasting life."*

Regardless of past beliefs, doubts, or circumstances, please believe the Scriptures and receive God's love. The Father loves you so much that He gave His Son for you that you may not perish, but have everlasting life. When we receive the Father's love for ourselves, we will begin to love Him and others. *"We love Him because He first loved us. If someone says, 'I love God' and hates his brother, he is a liar; for he who does not love his brother whom he has seen, how can he love God whom he has not seen? And this commandment we have from Him: that he who loves God must love his brother also"* (1 John 4:19-21).

35

The foremost characteristic of a Christian is to live in love. We are not able to love others (or ourselves) until we understand and receive our Lord's love for us first.

RECEIVE AND PUT ON LOVE

Don't listen to Satan, the world, people, or even your own thoughts if the message you are receiving undermines the truth of how much you are loved by God. Pray right now and thank Him for His love for you.

In 1 Corinthians 13:1-3 Paul said that if he did not have love, he had become nothing—and his acts would profit him nothing in God's Kingdom. This certainly applies to us.

The Bible says no matter how gifted, knowledgeable, generous or sacrificial we are, if we do not love, our works will profit us nothing and we will become nothing. Wow! This obviously foundational doctrine and characteristic is of utmost eternal consequence. Being loved by God and loving God and others is vital in our Christianity!

The two greatest commandments in Scripture are found in Matthew 22:36-40: *"'Teacher, which is the great commandment in the law?' Jesus said to him, 'You shall **love** the Lord your God with all your heart, with all your soul, and with all your mind.' This is the first and great commandment. And the second is like it: 'You shall **love** your neighbor as yourself.' On these two commandments hang all the Law and the Prophets."*

We are to be rooted and grounded in love (Ephesians 3:17-19). Because of His forgiveness to us, we are above all—to *put on* love (Colossians 3:14; 1 Peter 4:8). When we put on love, we will love people—even our enemies (Luke 6:35; 1 John 4:7-12). How would you evaluate your love for God and others?

ABOUNDING LOVE

Everything we do for Christ needs to be motivated by our love for Him (1 Corinthians 16:13-14, Galatians 5:6). His marvelous love compels us to Live on Target!

Please note how God's call to love will affect our appointment with Him on judgment day. *"Whoever confesses that Jesus is the Son of God, God abides in him, and he in God. And we have known and believed the love that God has for us. God is love, and he who abides in **love** abides in God, and God in him. Love has been perfected among us in this: that we may have boldness in the day of judgment"* (1 John 4:15-17).

The Apostle Paul shares this desire: *"And this I pray, that your **love** may abound still more and more in knowledge and all discernment, that you may approve the things that are excellent, that you may be sincere and without offense till the day of Christ, being filled with the fruits of righteousness which are by Jesus Christ, to the glory and praise of God"* (Philippians 1:9-11).

In 1 Thessalonians 3:12-13 we read this exhortation: *"And may the Lord make you increase and abound in **love** to one another and to all, just as we do to you, so that He may establish your hearts blameless in holiness before our God and Father at the coming of our Lord Jesus Christ with all His saints."*

Wow! According to these Scriptures, our love for God and others will greatly affect our judgment experience with Him when He returns. Will your heart be blameless in this area of love? Please receive God's love for yourself and then give it away. You won't regret it! May we all become established in His love!

2. GRACE

The Father is gracious and the Lord Jesus embodies grace and truth (Psalm 145:8 and John 1:14).

The word grace itself fills us with hope. Why? Because it is God's goodness and kindness poured out on us that cascades into our lives from the very heart of the Almighty Himself. Grace is God's unmerited favor and provision for our life and salvation.

God's grace is never deserved—always unmerited —but always lavished on His children in outrageous love and delight.

We can never wrap our minds fully around the miracle of grace. It is a truth that we begin to appropriate at salvation and then continue to discover, revel in, and respond to all the days of our walk here on earth. The grace of God saves us and offers us continual forgiveness for confessed sin. It also empowers us to live godly lives. Please receive the wonderful grace God offers you. Pray right now, thanking Him for His amazing grace toward you.

Evaluate how you are actively living out God's grace in your life toward Him and others.

THE DIVINE MOTIVATOR

God's grace toward us in all its fullness—naturally results in response. How tempting it is to read our favorite grace passages without looking at the full context. For example, Titus 2:11 records, *"For the grace of God that brings salvation has appeared to all men."* Wonderful! But don't stop there. In the very next breath Paul states, *"It [grace] teaches us to say 'No' to ungodliness and worldly passions, and to live self-controlled, upright and godly lives in this present age, while we wait for the blessed hope—the glorious appearing of our great God and Savior, Jesus Christ, who gave himself for us to redeem us from all wickedness and to purify for himself a people that are his very own, eager to do what is good"* (verses 12-14 NIV).

Grace results in response! This is a consistent pattern in Scripture. Ephesians 2:8-9 explains, *"For by grace you have been saved through faith, and that not of yourselves; it is the gift of God, not of works, lest anyone should boast."* Amen! But keep on reading! *"For we are His workmanship, created in Christ Jesus for good works, which God prepared beforehand that we should walk in them"* (verse 10).

Grace is a wonderful motivator for hitting the target of being well pleasing to God.

LIVING FROM THE INSIDE OUT

Second Corinthians 5:17 says, *"Therefore, if anyone is in Christ, he is a new creation; old things have passed away;*

behold, all things have become new."

After you place your faith in Christ alone for your salvation, you are a brand new creature! Your spirit desires to obey the Lord but your flesh does not. (The flesh is that part of us that rebels against the Spirit of God.) That is why Paul instructs us to walk in the Holy Spirit so that we will not gratify the desires of the flesh (Galatians 5:16).

The new you is now very much alive to God and dead to sin (Romans 6:11). This means that sin is no longer your master. The Scriptures do not say you will never sin, but according to Romans 6:7, you died to sin as your controlling influence. You will still be tempted, but you are no longer in bondage to sin because of Christ's life within you. He has given you the power over sin and you now have the privilege to live from the inside out; His life being lived through you!

YOUR IDENTITY IN CHRIST

Many people are trying to answer the question, "Who am I?" In fact, some of us search our entire lives attempting to answer this question. We often look to our parents, our performance, or our profession to define our identity. But all fall short.

The best place to discover the answer is to look to God and His Word. The first thing He tells us about our identity is that it is "in Christ." This phrase is repeated over and over in the New Testament. When we start watching for it we will be amazed at who we are—and what we have—in Christ.

Those who repent and place their faith in Christ become

first and foremost sons and daughters of God. This is our identity! John 1:12 says, *"But as many as received Him, to them He gave the right to become children of God, to those who believe in His name."*

This is exciting because before we were a child of our heavenly Father, we were His enemies (Romans 5:10). Now He has crucified and buried the ones who were His enemies and has resurrected us as His children. This is also known as the new birth as described in John 3.

You became "born again" the moment you were saved. Do you accept the fact that as a Christian your primary identity is as a son or daughter of God? Please believe and accept it.

HOLY AND RIGHTEOUS?

As Christians, not only are we children of God, we are saints ("holy") in Christ! The New Testament refers to us as saints more than sixty times. Apparently God wanted us to internalize that fact! Some might comment, "If I am a saint, then the Church is in a whole lot of trouble!"

We should all realize that we have flesh and that we have the capacity to sin. Our flesh might rebel at the thought of us being called saints, but this is exactly how the Bible describes us.

We received our sainthood (or holiness) from Christ when we received Him as our Lord and Savior. We did nothing to deserve or earn it. Again...*grace!* At our conversion (new birth) our old self was crucified with Christ so we would no longer live for ourselves—yet Christ would live His holy life in

41

and through us (Galatians 2:20). We received His identity as holy and righteous. This is truly the Great Exchange; your old life for the life of Christ!

In the world, a person's *behavior* determines his identity. In God's Kingdom, identity is determined by a person's *birth (conversion).*

Your first birth determined that you were a sinner. Your second birth has determined that you are a saint in Christ. Why? Because at your second birth, you became identified with Christ—and He is the Holy One! Christ takes up residence in you and you take on His identity. He becomes your "hope of glory." As the Bible confirms, *"God willed to make known what are the riches of the glory of this mystery among the Gentiles: which is Christ in you, the hope of glory"* (Colossians 1:27).

GOD'S GIFT TO YOU

Your position and identity—having been *"accepted in the Beloved"* (Ephesians 1:6). You are pronounced clean and holy!

One of the greatest truths the Holy Spirit will ever show you is that you became righteous in and through Christ Jesus at the moment you were saved. According to Scripture, *"For He made Him who knew no sin to be sin for us, that we might become the righteousness of God in Him"* (2 Corinthians 5:21).

Look closely at this verse. It tells us that God the Father made Jesus to become sin in our place. He took all of our transgressions upon Himself at the cross. Upon our repentance from sin and placing our faith in Him alone, the righteousness of the Almighty was imparted—and we became the righteousness of God in Christ! Wow! We did not deserve or earn this righteousness. It (like salvation) was a gift given to us at conversion (Romans 5:17). Again...grace!

Satan will persevere in tempting us to believe the opposite about ourselves. He tempts us to doubt God, our salvation and our identity in Christ. He loves to accuse us daily of many things (Revelation 12:10-11) and bring us into condemnation. He tempts us to believe that we are failures, that we never quite measure up, that we're not valuable enough, etc. Don't believe his deceit! The devil is the father of lies (John 8:44).

If we are being tempted to sin or feel condemned, we know that those thoughts are not from God (James 1:13; Romans 8:1). Godly sorrow (redemptive conviction) comes from God. Condemnation does not—for those who are walking in the Spirit. Reject and replace any lies of the enemy with the truth of who you are in Christ Jesus.

No one can control the initial thoughts that enter our minds (Oh, how we wish we could!), but we do have control of them after they arrive. We can either entertain the thoughts or take them captive to the obedience of Christ (2 Corinthians 10:3-5). Take them captive and walk in victory!

From this day forward, protect your thought life and make a distinction between lies and truth. We are the righteousness of God in Christ! Praise Him!

We know that the Father highly values our obedience (which pleases Him), but not for the purpose of making us more righteous. *Only He can make us righteous,* and He has already done that in Christ. Again...*amazing grace!*

ABIDING IN CHRIST

We are never asked to live the Christian life in our own strength. That is impossible! Jesus said, *"Abide in Me, and I in you. As the branch cannot bear fruit of itself, unless it abides in the vine, neither can you, unless you abide in Me. I am the vine, you are the branches. He who abides in Me, and I in him, bears much fruit; for <u>without Me you can do nothing</u>"* (John 15: 4-5).

As we abide (remain) in Christ and develop intimacy with Him, He empowers us with the fruit of the Spirit—which is love, joy, peace, longsuffering, kindness, goodness, faithfulness, gentleness, self-control—and also a fruitful life of service. Does this describe you? Christians should be the most loving, joyful and servant-minded people on the entire planet! This kind of lifestyle brings glory and pleasure to God the Father and testifies that we are His disciples. *"By this My Father is glorified, that you bear much fruit; so you will be my disciples"* (John 15:6).

YOUR ALL IN ALL

Many of you know that Jesus is your Lord and Savior. But do you understand that Jesus is your Life?

Scripture declares, *"When <u>Christ who is our life</u> appears, then you also will appear with Him in glory"* (Colossians 3:4). What does it mean for Christ to be your Life? This tells us He is your ultimate Source. Your All in All. He is the means by which you live.

In practical terms, Jesus Christ desires to live His life through you every day. He wants to express Himself this way personally.

This in no way wipes out your personality, which God has uniquely given to you, but He wants to use your words and actions to present Himself to the world.

Even more, Jesus Christ living through you is the only way you will be able to live a life that is pleasing to God. The Holy Spirit who resides in you is there to lead and to fill you with the life of Christ so that you will have the necessary power to obey the Lord and to please Him. In fact, this is the only way you can give joy and delight to your heavenly Father.

TO LIVE IS CHRIST

If you try to obey God the Father without allowing Christ to live through you, your obedience will have no eternal value. This means there will be no reward. Any works performed through the flesh (works that do not originate with dependence on Jesus Christ) will be wood, hay and straw. They will burn at the Judgment Seat of Christ (1 Corinthians 3:12-15).

Just as it is necessary to pray that God's will be done in your life, you need to ask Jesus Christ to live through you—for this is definitely God's will.

The Apostle Paul wrote in Philippians 1:21: *"For to me, to live is Christ, and to die is gain."* What did Paul mean, *"to live is Christ"*? He determined that every day of his journey, he was so dependent on Christ to live through him, it was actually Christ who was manifesting Himself through Paul's daily walk.

Can you say the same thing? Are you so dependent on the Lord that you too can declare, "To live is Christ"?

Paul stated, *"For I will not dare to speak of any of those things <u>which Christ has not accomplished through me</u>, in word and deed, to make the Gentiles obedient"* (Romans 15:18). The apostle was clear that the only things which really mattered to him—the only accomplishments he cared about—were what Christ had carried out through him.

The basis of your freedom in Christ is Jesus living His life through you. This is why you can exclaim with Paul, *"I have been crucified with Christ; it is no longer I who live, but <u>Christ lives in me</u>; and the life which I now live in the flesh I live by faith in the Son of God, who loved me and gave Himself for me"* (Galatians 2:20).

Again we have Paul clearly stating that He was relying on Christ to be his very life.

FREEDOM!

The Bible teaches us that we are no longer dominated or enslaved by sin and we have been given the power through the Holy Spirit to live in freedom and righteousness (Romans 6:17-18). Why then do we continue to experience a spiritual war within us?

Paul, with tremendous transparency, described his own battle with the law of sin that remained in him after his conversion (Romans 7:14-25). He openly admitted that there were times in his life that he did not do the good that he wanted, but would end up doing some things that he hated. Can you identify with Paul? We all can, because we all have this law of sin within our flesh which is constantly warring against the Holy Spirit who also lives inside us.

Before salvation, we had no power to overcome sin in our life...and sin dominated us. At our conversion, we were sealed and empowered by the Holy Spirit and thus given the ability to live in freedom and righteousness.

"I say then: <u>Walk in the Spirit, and you shall not fulfill the lust of the flesh</u>. For the flesh lusts against the Spirit, and the Spirit against the flesh; and these are contrary to one another, so that you do not do the things that you wish" (Galatians 5:16-17). Notice that our responsibility is to walk in the Spirit. The word "walk" means to "live in," "be occupied with," or "to regulate one's life by."

If we walk in the Spirit of God we will not fulfill the desires of the flesh and we will bear the fruit of the Spirit (Galatians 5:22-23)—which of course pleases our Lord. Walking in the Spirit does not free us from the temptation of sin. It frees us from the power of sin.

The key to a fruitful life is daily surrender to Christ and the powerful Holy Spirit within us. Our surrender brings us FREEDOM! Freedom from the domination of sin, freedom from religious bondage, freedom from legalism, and freedom from condemnation. We now have freedom to love, freedom to receive and extend forgiveness, freedom to experience His healing, freedom to worship, and freedom to serve our Lord with joy, passion and thanksgiving.

Our ultimate liberty will be experienced when we receive our sin-free, flesh-free bodies at the resurrection (1 Corinthians 15). We will one day experience heaven and live without the battle of sin and flesh. What a day to look forward to! Until then…walk in the Spirit and live your life from the inside out.

The grace of God has given us salvation, a new identity, power over sin and a brand new FREEDOM! May we use this divine grace to serve Him with reverence and godly fear as we anticipate our appointment with Him.

3. FEARING A HOLY GOD

"Therefore, since we are receiving a kingdom which cannot be shaken, let us have grace, by which we may serve God acceptably with reverence and <u>godly fear</u>. For our God is a consuming fire" (Hebrews 12:28-29), *"…as He who called you is holy, you also be holy in all your conduct, because it is written, 'Be holy, <u>for I am holy</u>'"* (1 Peter 1:15-16).

Paul understood that there are many facets of God's character. Although our gracious heavenly Father certainly is love, He is also a holy consuming fire. God is loving, gracious and holy…at the same time!

In 2 Corinthians 5:11 Paul states that he had come to know the fear of the Lord. Because of his maturity in understanding this, he gave his life to persuade others to reconcile with God and to prepare to meet Him face to face. He was concerned that the fear of God had been lost and he stated that fact in Romans 3:18: *"There is no fear of God before their eyes."* The word "fear" is translated "terror, reverence, respect and honor."

Earlier in Romans 1, Paul listed some of the traits that characterized the godless people of the day. Among other things, he said that they were "immoral, full of envy, strife, deceit, violent, proud, inventors of evil things, disobedient to parents, undiscerning, untrustworthy, unloving, unforgiving, and unmerciful."

Sad to say, I believe we can identify with Paul's concern and echo these same words to describe our society today. The very things that should cause us to tremble before a holy God and repent, have been minimized or even ignored. In fact, there are many people claiming to be born again Christians, but their lifestyles aren't any different than nonbelievers'. We simply cannot live a life of sin without conviction and then say that we fear God. *"...by the fear of the Lord one departs from evil"* (Proverbs 16:6). The biblical fear of God needs to be taught, understood and practiced by the present church.

The early church practiced this understanding and grew because of it. As the churches were, *"...walking in the fear of the Lord and in the comfort of the Holy Spirit, they were multiplied"* (Acts 9:31).

The two keys to the churches' growth and maturity were; walking in the fear of the Lord, and walking in the comfort of the Holy Spirit. These two keys bring us freedom and power to be the sons and daughters of God that He has called us to be. Walking this way strengthens us not to fear anyone or anything else. *"For God has not given us a spirit of fear, but of power and of love and of a sound mind"* (2 Timothy 1:7).

Oh, that His church today would return to living out this truth...because <u>He is still holy!</u>
   Please note the following passages:

- Psalm 2:11: *"Serve the Lord <u>with fear</u> and rejoice with trembling."*

- Psalm 25:14: *"The secret of the Lord is with those who <u>fear Him</u>, And He will show them His covenant."*

- Psalm 103:13,17 (NIV): *"As a father has compassion on those who <u>fear him</u>...But from everlasting to everlasting the LORD's love is with those who <u>fear him</u>..."*

- Psalm 128:1: *"Blessed is every one who <u>fears the LORD</u>, Who walks in His ways."*

- Luke 1:50: *"And His mercy is on those who <u>fear Him</u> from generation to generation."*

- Luke 12:5: *"But I will show you whom you should fear: <u>Fear Him</u> who, after He has killed, has power to cast into hell; yes, I say to you, <u>fear Him</u>!"*

- 2 Corinthians 7:1: *"Therefore, having these promises, beloved, let us cleanse ourselves from all filthiness of the flesh and spirit, perfecting holiness in <u>the fear of God</u>."*

- 1 Peter 2:17: *"Honor all people. Love the brother-hood. <u>Fear God</u>. Honor the king."*

- Revelation 14:7: *"<u>Fear God</u> and give glory to Him, for the hour of His judgment has come; and worship Him who made heaven and earth, the sea and springs of water."*

Solomon, at the conclusion of his life came to the same resolve. *"Let us hear the conclusion of the whole matter: Fear God and keep His commandments, for this is man's all. For God will bring every work into judgment, including every secret thing, whether good or evil"* (Ecclesiastes 12:13-14).

I hope that we begin to appreciate what all of these Scriptures mean and that we gain wisdom about His character.

May we fear God and give Him glory as we anticipate His return. He is still holy and just...and must be revered as such!

Because of the Apostle Paul's understanding of the character of God and the judgment to come, he gave his life in order to urge and persuade the Church to prepare for that day when they would meet Him face to face. He articulated very clearly that he knew the fear, or the terror of the Lord. Do you know Him in this way?

GOD'S CHARACTER NEVER CHANGES

There is a difference between the old and the new covenants, but not in the *God* of these covenants. There is not a God of the old covenant (Old Testament) and a different God of the new covenant (New Testament). He is one and the same and His character has never changed and never will.

Some mistakenly believe that God was not merciful and gracious under the old covenant, but Exodus 34:6-7 states the opposite: *"...The Lord, the Lord God, merciful and gracious, longsuffering, and abounding in goodness and truth, keeping mercy for thousands, forgiving iniquity and transgression and sin by no means clearing the guilty..."*

God has always been merciful, gracious, loving and forgiving. At the same time, He has always been holy and just. If we don't confess and repent of our sin, He will by no means clear the guilty.

In Proverbs 9:10, Scripture declares, *"The <u>fear of the Lord</u> is the beginning of wisdom, and the knowledge of the Holy One is understanding."* To gain wisdom, we must begin with understanding...accepting and submitting to the total character of God.

<u>We serve the Lord because of our love for Him, but our fear (or respect and reverence) of God should also drive us away from sin and to Him</u>, cleansing ourselves from all filthiness of our flesh and spirit, perfecting holiness in the <u>fear of God</u> (See 2 Corinthians 7:1).

Pray right now, thanking Him for being a holy God worthy of your reverential fear. Evaluate your biblical fear of a holy God and how you are living this out with Him and others.

THE JUDGMENT OF GOD

Jesus said, *"...For judgment I have come into this world..."* (John 9:39). A judgment day is coming for all of us.

I believe we need to pause and contemplate what this truly means. It is essential that we stop and allow this fact to penetrate our hearts and minds: Every person on the planet will one day stand before a very holy God and will not only give an account of their life, but will experience either everlasting punishment or eternal life. *"And these will go away into everlasting punishment, but the righteous into eternal life"* (Matthew 25:46). Please notice the words "everlasting" and "eternal"…it never ends! Wow! Are you ready for your appointment with God?

The reality of this day of accounting should in and of itself shake us, wake us, and cause us to evaluate and repent. It should make us passionately determined to live a surrendered and holy life that will be well pleasing to God.

The Apostle Peter wrote, *"For the time has come for judgment to begin at the house of God; and if it begins with us first, what will be the end of those who do not obey the gospel of God? Now 'If the righteous one is scarcely saved, Where will the ungodly and the sinner appear?'"* (1 Peter 4:17-18).

What awaits the ungodly and the sinner? Peter answers this in 2 Peter 3:7: *"But the heavens and the earth which are now preserved by the same word, are reserved for fire until the day of judgment and perdition of ungodly men."* The Apostle Paul also answers this question very clearly in 2 Thessalonians 1:5-9: *"…which is manifest evidence of the righteous judgment of God, that you may be counted worthy of the kingdom of God, for which you also suffer; since it is a righteous thing with God to repay with tribulation those* who trouble you, and to give you who are troubled rest with us when the Lord Jesus is revealed from heaven with His mighty angels, _in flaming fire taking vengeance on those who do not know God, and on those who do not obey the gospel of our Lord Jesus Christ. These shall be punished with everlasting destruction from the presence of the Lord and from the glory of His power._"

The Apostle John adds, "_Then I saw a great white throne and Him who sat on it, from whose face the earth and the heaven fled away. And there was found no place for them. And I saw the dead, small and great, standing before God, and books were opened. And another book was opened, which is the Book of Life. And the dead were judged according to their works, by the things which were written in the books. The sea gave up the dead who were in it, and Death and Hades delivered up the dead who were in them. And they were judged, each one according to his works. Then Death and Hades were cast into the lake of fire. This is the second death. And anyone not found written in the Book of Life was cast into the lake of fire_" (Revelation 20:11-15).

Jesus and the apostles Peter, Paul, and John all refer to this extremely horrific and sobering judgment that awaits all nonbelievers. This judgment should convict and move every Christian to share the Gospel at all cost. It is a matter of eternal life or death!

If your name is in the Lamb's Book of Life by faith in Christ, thank Him this very moment! If your name is not written in the Lamb's Book of Life, please consider this: Christ paid the price for your sin on the cross. Confess that you have sinned, repent and by faith receive His payment on your behalf. You will receive His righteousness in exchange for your debt of sin. You will then stand in His righteousness on the day of judgment.

A DAY OF ACCOUNTING

Thankfully, on one hand, many of us do know that our names are in the Book of Life by faith alone in Christ, but on the other hand we don't seem to have the proper level of fear or respect for our own appointment with God. Hear the words of Peter, *"And if you call on the Father, who without partiality judges according to each one's work, conduct yourselves throughout the time of your stay here in fear"* (1 Peter 1:17).

Paul also cited his reason for aiming to please God in 2 Corinthians 5:10-11, *"For we must all appear before the Judgment Seat of Christ that each one may receive the things done in the body, according to what he has done, whether good or bad. Knowing, therefore, the terror (fear) of the Lord, we persuade men."*

As Christians, how we carry out our lives here is obviously *very important* to God. The Lord did not save us only for heaven, but also to make a spiritual impact while we are here on this earth.

The fruit of how we live now will be brought to light at the Judgment Seat of Christ. Many Christians may not be taking this appointment seriously, yet Paul certainly did, and so should we.

The Bible is very clear that we will give an account to God and that He will indeed judge us for what we did with His gift of salvation. Romans 5:9 and 1 Thessalonians 5:9 explain that we are saved from the wrath of God. Praise the Lord!

However, we are not exempt from giving an account of our lives to God. The Bible is clear; The Lord will judge His people. And judgment begins at the house of God (Hebrews 10:30 and 1 Peter 4:17).

This judgment is also mentioned by Paul in Romans 14:10-12: *"You, then, why do you judge your brother? Or why do you look down on your brother? For we will all stand before God's judgment seat. It is written: 'As surely as I live,' says the Lord, 'every knee will bow before me; every tongue will confess to God.' So then, <u>each of us will give an account</u> of himself to God"* (NIV).

Hebrews 4:13 says, *"And there is no creature hidden from His sight, but all things are naked and open to the eyes of Him to whom we must give account."* And in 1 Corinthians 3:11-15, we read, *"For no other foundation can anyone lay than that which is laid, which is Jesus Christ. Now if anyone builds on this foundation with gold, silver, precious stones, wood, hay, straw, each one's work will become clear; for the Day will declare it, because it will be revealed by fire; and the fire will test each one's work, of what sort it is. If anyone's work which he has built on it endures, he will receive a reward. If anyone's work is burned, he will suffer loss; but he himself will be saved, yet so as through fire."*

We also need to read 1 Corinthians 4:4-5: *"My conscience is clear, but that does not make me innocent. <u>It is the Lord who judges</u> me. Therefore judge nothing before the appointed time; wait till the Lord comes. He will bring to light what is hidden in darkness and will expose the <u>motives of men's hearts</u>. At that time each will receive his praise from God"* (NIV).

This judgment is indeed for Christians. It is not a question of salvation, but one of heart motives, attitudes, fruitfulness, works, stewardship, rewards and responsibilities in eternity (Matthew 25:14-30, Luke 19:11-27, 1 Corinthians 3:11-15). May we prepare ourselves to meet Him face to face. Use us Lord, for your glory!

REWARDS

"For the Son of Man will come in the glory of His Father with His angels, and then <u>He will reward</u> each according to his works" (Matthew 16:27).

We may not think that being rewarded for our faith is necessary, but it is obviously what our Lord desires to do for His children. Just like earthly parents enjoy giving to and rewarding their children, God delights to do this for us. Jesus said, *"And behold, I am coming quickly, and <u>My reward is with Me, to give to every one according to his work</u>"* (Revelation 22:12). Jesus also declared, *"Behold, I am coming quickly! Hold fast what you have, that no one may take your crown"* (Revelation 3:11).

The Apostle John counsels: *"Look to yourselves, that we do not lose <u>those things we worked for, but that we may receive a full reward</u>"* (2 John 1:8).

Jesus even desires to repay us for ministering to people who cannot repay us on earth (Luke 14:13-14). Amazing! The heart of our Lord is to reward His children for their obedience. He is the rewarder (Hebrews 11:6).

If God desires to give rewards then we should desire to receive them from Him. This is not selfish ambition, but holy ambition. We must release ourselves to receive from God whatever He desires to give us.

The following crowns are mentioned in the New Testament.

1. Crown of Life—given for love and faithfulness to Christ and/or martyrdom (James 1:12; Revelation 2:10).

2. Imperishable Crown—given for spiritual discipline and perseverance in the Christian life (1 Corinthians 9:24-25).

3. Crown of Rejoicing—given for pouring oneself into others through evangelism and discipleship (This reward could be the people themselves.) (1 Thessalonians 2:19; Philippians 4:1).

4. Crown of Glory—given for faithfully representing Christ through a function of spiritual leadership (1 Peter 5:1-4).

5. Crown of Righteousness—given for preparing oneself and others to meet Christ by loving and expecting His appearing (His return) (2 Timothy 4:6-8).

Our ultimate reward, of course, is Christ Himself. Any crowns that we receive will bring glory to Him. In Revelation 4:10 we have an example of what we may do with our crowns: *"...the twenty-four elders fall down before Him who sits on the throne and worship Him who lives forever and ever, and cast their crowns before the throne."* This example shows that our rewards are not given merely for our recognition —but for God's glory.

Consider the words of Randy Alcorn: "Although God's glory is the highest reason for any action, Scripture sees no contradiction between God's eternal glory and our eternal good. On the contrary, glorifying God will always result in our greatest eternal good. Likewise, pursuing our eternal good as He commands us to do...will always glorify God."

If it doesn't seem "spiritual" to desire God's rewards; if it seems self-centered...then let Scripture override your hesitation. God wants to reward us. You have the freedom to whole-heartedly embrace the fact that He wants to reward His children.

If you're living your life on target for Him, keeping your relationship pure, serving Him from your heart...then you can enthusiastically receive the rewards He so desires to give you...all for His glory!

A CALL TO HOLINESS

Many make the mistake of believing it doesn't really matter how we live on earth because we have been saved by grace. We're going to heaven and we are claiming grace even though some of us are living just like the world. We don't seem to be very motivated to mature in our faith! Yet Paul stated, *"The grace of God teaches us that denying ungodliness and worldly lust, we should live soberly, righteously and godly in this present age"* (Titus 2:11-12).

59

The grace of God, in all its glory and beauty, never undermines His call to holiness.

It *does* matter how we live as Christians in this present world, and it matters greatly. It is very possible that countless tears will be shed at the Judgment Seat of Christ and some of us will be *"saved...as through fire"* (1 Corinthians 3:15)—but will experience shame and loss of rewards for how we lived our lives before Him.

Please remember that although God will never love us more than He does right now, how we live our lives affects our ability to experience and enjoy that love. His unchanging and powerful love for us by no means takes away from the importance of our appointment with Him. Our righteous Judge will reward our obedience and will judge our works and motives.

Ultimately, there will be no shame, pain, or death in His eternal Kingdom...and He graciously will wipe away every tear from our eyes (Revelation 2:14). There really is no need to experience shame on Judgment Day. We have all been warned about the coming judgment and empowered to abide in Him so that we may have confidence at His coming. *"And now, little children, abide in Him, that when He appears, we may have confidence and not be ashamed before Him at His coming"* (1 John 2:28).

Fellow believers, we can Live on Target and be well pleasing to God, both now and at the Judgment Seat of Christ. May we live our lives with <u>no regrets</u>!

We are grateful to our Lord for His love that He lavishes upon us and with which He pursues us. We should be extremely thankful for the grace of God. None of us would be saved without it! Yet neither the love of God nor His grace should be used as an excuse by Christians to live an aimless life. Instead, we can live with purpose, joy, and sacrifice, laboring for the Kingdom with proper motives and stewardship.

THE GOODNESS AND SEVERITY OF GOD

Consider the words of John Bevere in his book, *The Fear of the Lord:*

> Paul ...wrote, *"In the last days there will be very difficult times. For people will love only themselves and their money. They will be boastful and proud, scoffing at God, disobedient to their parents, and ungrateful. They will consider nothing sacred. They will be unloving and unforgiving; they will slander others and have no self-control; they will be cruel and have no interest in what is good. They will betray their friends, be reckless, be puffed up with pride, and love pleasure rather than God"* (2 Timothy 3:1-4, NLT).
>
> *The most somber truth is that Paul is not describing society but the church, for he continues: "they will act as if they are religious, but they will reject the power that could make them godly" (2 Timothy 3:5, NLT). They will frequently attend church, hear God's Word, talk God's Word, boast in the saving grace of the Lord, but will reject the power that could make them godly.*
>
> *What is the power that could make them godly? The answer is simple: It is the very grace of God of which they boast.*

For the past twenty to thirty years, the grace taught and believed in many of our churches is not real grace, but a perversion of it. This is the result of overemphasizing the <u>goodness</u> of God to the neglect of the <u>fear</u> of Him.

When the doctrine of the love of God is not balanced with an understanding of the fear of God, error is the result. Likewise, when the fear of God is not balanced by the love of God, we have the same results. This is why we are exhorted to <u>"consider the goodness and severity of God"</u> (Romans 11:22). It takes both—and without both, we end up unbalanced.

May we seriously consider this as we anticipate the Judgment Seat of Christ. We have a tendency in the Church to elevate one aspect of truth over others. When we do, we become theologically and practically unbalanced.

We must accept and apply <u>all</u> of God's Word and His character to our lives. As we have read in this chapter, God's <u>love</u>, <u>grace</u> and <u>holiness</u> should empower and motivate us all to live a faithful Christian life. We will give an account to Him. This is one appointment that none of us will be late for; one we are sure to keep.

I pray we stay ever mindful of our inevitable face to face meeting with God. It is something that we can, indeed, look forward to if we are living a life that is well pleasing to Him.

REEVALUATE YOUR PRIORITIES

If you are not a Christian, I implore you to receive Jesus

Christ today as your Lord and Savior. This is the most important relationship available to mankind! Jesus is the only way to the Heavenly Father. John 14:6 puts it this way, *"Jesus said to him, 'I am the way, the truth, and the life. No one comes to the Father except through Me.'"*

Christ will free you from the penalty of sin. *"For the wages of sin is death, but the gift of God is eternal life in Christ Jesus our Lord"* (Romans 6:23). Pause right now, confess that you are a sinner, repent and by faith, receive the free gift of salvation He offers. You will begin your new life in Him. He hears the prayers of repentant people.

You will not only begin the most rewarding journey on this earth, you will go to heaven and you will also avoid the Lake of Fire.

If you are already a believer, let me encourage you to reevaluate your priorities in light of your personal appointment with God at the Judgment Seat of Christ.

As Randy Alcorn writes in his book, *The Law of Rewards:* *"Five minutes after we die every Christian will understand that heaven is our home and earth was simply a temporary lodging on the homeward journey. Then we'll know for certain what was important and what wasn't. We will see with eternity's clarity. We will know exactly how we should have lived. But we don't have to wait until we die to know how we should live. God has given us his Word to tell us how to live and his indwelling Spirit to empower us to live as we should."*

And he adds, *"We can either take off the blinders now, while we still have our earthly lives to live, or wait for them to be taken off after death—when it will be too late to go back and change what we've done on earth. May what will be most important to us five minutes after we die become most important to us now."*

Let us humble ourselves before God with a desire and passion to please him. *"A broken and a contrite heart—these, O God, You will not despise"* (Psalm 51:17).

What you are about to read in the following chapters is not a checklist or a program to follow, but a lifestyle—one that will bring delight to the Father and will enable each of us to live a fruitful and joyful life on this earth while we wait for His return.

As children of God, we please Him when we live and serve out of love, grace and godly fear. These characteristics need to be our motivators for Living on Target.

REFLECT AND RESPOND

- Do you really believe you will stand before God one day? Why?

- In what ways are you challenged to adjust your beliefs and perspectives on God's love, grace and holiness? How would these adjustments affect your daily life?

- Are you prepared to see God face to face and does your lifestyle reflect it?

- What changes need to be made in your life (or things to be placed in order) before you personally meet God?

If the Holy Spirit has challenged you concerning your upcoming appointment with God, pause for a moment. Tell the Father that you agree with His Word and desire to live a life according to His purpose and plan. Ask Him to prepare you as you continue to develop as one of His mature disciples.

> *God is always attracted to*
> *humility and brokenness.*

THREE

FOUNDATION #1

LIVING IN LOVE AND SERVICE TO CHRIST

I am the vine, you are the branches. He who abides in Me, and I in him, bears much fruit; for without Me you can do nothing.

– JOHN 15:5

God desires an intimate relationship with you! Before He wants your *service* unto Him, He just wants *you*. Please let this truth sink in.

This is the most important foundation of all. If you miss the fact that our Lord wants *you* first and foremost, then nothing of eternal value will be accomplished.

Herein lies the chasm between religion and relationship. God, in His amazing grace and love, calls us to a deep, abiding fellowship and communion with Him, the Savior of our souls.

May we enjoy our relationship with Him (Psalm 37:4)!

God, in His fullness, doesn't *need* a relationship with us. He *desires* one. *"God is love"* (1 John 4:16) and He so loved us that He sent His Son to die on a cross that we might have everlasting life. He desires a love relationship with us so much that the first commandment is: *"And you shall love the Lord your God with all your heart, with all your soul, with all your mind, and with all your strength"* (Mark 12:30; Deuteronomy 6:5).

As we read the Scriptures, we see that God will reward our proper motives and works performed in His name. Although this is true, there is something which is as significant to our Lord as our works for Him. It is keeping our hearts pure and in love with Him.

Christians can perform good works for the Lord and others, but miss the most essential ministry of all—their heart relationship with Him.

Pleasing God begins with receiving His love, which becomes the foundation from which our ministry to Him overflows in love and gratitude.

Our first ministry should be unto God before anyone else. To bless our Lord and to keep our hearts pure before Him, we must establish this ministry <u>first</u>.

<u>Our vertical relationship with God affects every horizontal relationship we have on this earth</u>. It affects how we treat people and deal with every situation we face in life. He is the source of life...draw from Him!

Let's look at some passages that specify God's call to a personal love relationship:

- God loves a broken, contrite and pure heart (Psalm 51:17, Matthew 5:8).

- Your Father wants you to pray (communicate) with Him privately (Matthew 6:6).

- God's primary command is a love relationship with Him and others (Matthew 22:36-40).

- First abide in love with Him. Remaining in relationship with Christ Jesus is the only way to accomplish anything of eternal value (John 15:1-6).

- Our faithful God actually *calls you* into fellowship with Christ. He wants *you* before He wants your *service* or *works* (1 Corinthians 1:9).

- Without love, our works profit nothing (1 Corinthians 13:1-3).

- The Lord promises to reward those who diligently seek *Him* (Hebrews 11:6).

- Our love of Christ must come before works (Revelation 2:1-5).

RECAPTURE YOUR FIRST LOVE

The people in the church at Ephesus forgot that Christ first wanted them in a love relationship with Him. This church was started by Paul and was a powerful witness for Christ —even performing many wonderful works. However, Christ Himself eventually became displeased. As we read in Revelation 2:1-5, even though they were working for Christ, they abandoned their first love (who was Jesus Christ Himself).

Many have fallen into this trap. This is why Jesus gave the church instructions regarding how to recapture Him as their first love. He told them to remember the place from which they had fallen and then to repent and do the first works. In other words, "Go back and do what you did at the start of our relationship together—the things that you did when you first fell in love with Me."

Do you remember what your relationship with God was like when He saved you?

- Were you thankful?
- Did you desire to worship Him with a grateful heart?
- Did you long to pray and read His Word?
- Was your baptism a passionate expression of your obedience and public declaration of your new walk with Him?

You knew He had cleansed and forgiven you. You wanted to be with Him and share His love with others.

Sadly, as time passes, we have a tendency to become distracted or even forget and fall away from the One who has given us life. This happened to the nation of Israel, to the church at Ephesus, and is occurring in many of us today.

This does not take place overnight. We begin to stray gradually. *"We must pay more careful attention...to what we have heard, <u>so that we do not drift away</u>"* (Hebrews 2:1 NIV).

In light of this warning, if this has happened to you, please follow the instructions of Jesus: Repent of this sin and begin doing those things that will keep you in love and fellowship with Him. James 4:8 states, *"Draw near to God and He will draw near to you."* Please notice that we are to draw near to Him and <u>then</u> He will draw near to us.

If we are not experiencing a closeness in our relationship with the Lord, it is because *we* have deviated from the path, not *Him.* God desires to see His sons and daughters taking the initiative to spend time in His presence.

He is not referring to location, but to fellowship. Our Lord lives in us but we can still neglect the relationship. John 15:4-5 tells us to abide in Christ and He will abide in us.

The word "abide" means to remain or to continue. He is saying that if we will remain in Him, He will remain in us and enable us to bear much fruit for the Kingdom.

Without Christ empowering us, how can we accomplish anything of eternal value? Remember the words of Jesus: *"...for without Me you can do nothing"* (John 15:5). If we ignore love and intimacy with our Lord, then everything else just becomes religious activity. We may do good deeds, but we will achieve nothing of lasting worth.

This foundation of living in relationship with the Lord simply cannot be violated or bypassed. It is a vital aspect of our Christian walk.

Let me share the following three spiritual disciplines in achieving intimacy with our Lord: Prayer, The Word, and Personal Worship.

1. Prayer

But you, when you pray, go into your room,
and when you have shut your door, pray to your
Father who is in the secret place; and your Father
who sees in secret will reward you openly.
– Matthew 6:6

I have come to believe that this verse is one of the most crucial verses in the entire Bible. Jesus is teaching us how to have closeness with our Heavenly Father. It is essential for each of us to find this "quiet place" to meet with God on a daily basis. Jesus uses the expression, *"When* you pray", not *"If* you pray." He repeats the same statement three times in this teaching on prayer.

The instruction to go into our room and shut the door is significant in light of our busy lifestyles. In the natural, we have a tendency to retreat from isolation and solitude and run toward people and "things"—toward television, computers, electronic devices, and other forms of distraction. Busyness and constant confusion is exactly what the enemy desires; to divert us from having any time of solitude with our Lord.

We need to learn how to become quiet before the Father so we will develop spiritually sensitive ears to hear what the

Spirit of God has to say. Prayer is not just talking to the Father, it is also *listening* to Him.

The primary barrier in most relationships (including our fellowship with the Lord) is not tied to our ability to talk, but our ability to listen. The Almighty declares, *"Be still, and know that I am God"* (Psalm 46:10).

Unfortunately, many of us do not hear the Lord speak to us, either in our spirit or through His Word, because we are not still or quiet long enough to hear His voice. We as Christians should recognize the voice of our Shepherd (John 10:3-4). To know God, we must spend time communicating with Him.

Being in isolation with the Lord provides an opportunity for us to develop intimacy with Him and spiritual ears to continuously hear what the Spirit is saying to us.

A TIME APART

I am constantly drawn to the statement Jesus made concerning going into our room and shutting the door.

Do you have a special place that is designated for you to meet with God? If not, I strongly encourage you to find one. In discipling people in this area, I've found there are a variety of "rooms" that people retreat to, not only inside a physical building, but also under the sky. Some are "outdoor" people and they love to find a quiet place with Him under a certain tree, or perhaps walking down a secluded path.

The exact location is not the main issue. The main issue is

finding and maintaining a quiet place where you can meet with God on a daily basis—where you can be alone with your Lord. He invites you to come to Him to get rest for your soul (Matthew 11:28-30). There is no better rest!

You can also *emotionally* close a door to the cares of the world: to what your schedule is like this morning, this afternoon, or tomorrow. You can lock yourself away from life's distractions and open up the door of your heart to the Lord. The quiet place is extremely necessary and the absolute key to living a life that is well pleasing to Him.

We can become so involved in activities, or even doing good works for the Lord, that we simply forfeit being in His presence, praying, reading His Word or personally worshiping Him. It's essential to be still enough to hear what He is saying to our spirit. The answers for our life's decisions and challenges are found here.

Be aware of thoughts, Scripture passages, ideas, people's names, clarity, revelations, dreams, understandings, or an abiding peace that you may experience. All of these could be the Lord speaking to your heart and mind.

<u>This place of solitude is critical</u>, but sad to say, it is an element most Christians may be missing. As a result of not meeting God regularly in a quiet place to hear from Him, there will be a lack of passion for the Lord, our families, the church, and for the lost.

The good news is that there is nothing impossible with God! So whatever troubles, challenges or struggles we have today, the Lord is the remedy—if we will just return to Him in an intimate way.

MOVE INTO HIS PRESENCE

There is no substitute for the presence of God in our lives. If we are feeling distant from the Lord or having trouble in our marriage, problems with our children, challenges with our finances, not satisfied with our attitudes, life's journey, issues in the church, whatever it may be—there is *nothing* God can't accomplish. If our circumstances remain the same, He will change and guide us through them! If we will move into His presence, *He will change our thoughts, vocabulary, behavior—our very lives.*

Scripture states that He is a rewarder of those who diligently seek Him (Hebrews 11:6). Why do we run toward people, books, and other resources instead of running first to the Lord? God is the change agent and our rewarder, not people. Others can certainly pray for and encourage us (we need that), but they themselves cannot change us. God is the one who has the ability to transform our hearts and lives. May we take God at His Word when He says that He rewards us for pursuing Him.

He does so with His presence, wisdom, comfort, healing, peace, direction—and so much more. Diligently seeking Him is certainly to our advantage. He delights in our pursuit of Him!

Remember, "Draw near to God and He will draw near to you!" Where? And How? In that quiet location where you listen, pray, read His Word, and worship. This is the "quiet place" where the noise and disturbances of the day can be brushed to the side and your heart can turn to God alone. It is a vital element in experiencing His presence on a consistent basis.

HE HAS CAPTURED MY HEART

One young disciple put it this way, "I have become protective of that 'alone time' with Him. When I make God the very center of my life and allow Him to pour into me, every other aspect of life is affected by Him—and a steady reflection of God begins to shine through. *I cannot stand in the presence of God and not be changed.*"

This individual had participated with a group studying the material you are now reading, and commented, "Living on Target, and the person who mentored me along the way, have led me to the feet of Jesus and *He* has captured my heart. It is something which constantly takes me to a deeper place in my faith and draws me closer to Him in my walk."

There is no possible way to achieve biblical order in our lives unless we establish an intimate relationship with Him in our quiet place. He is the foundation upon which every other relationship or event along our journey should be built. When this is established, then and only then can any of us begin to exhibit a victorious and fruitful life.

A nineteenth century evangelist from South Africa, Andrew Murray, stated, "I have learned to place myself before God every day as a vessel to be filled with the Holy Spirit. If there is one lesson that I am learning day by day, it is this...that it is God who worketh all in all."

OUR MODEL PRAYER

In this quiet place, our Lord is calling us to perhaps the greatest discipline in the Christian life—prayer. It is also one

76

of our foremost challenges.

Jesus did not leave us without instruction on how to pray. He taught us what is known today as The Lord's Prayer.

The words were not intended to simply be recited. It is a model prayer which we can use to communicate with our Father. Here is how Jesus taught us to pray: *"Our Father in heaven, hallowed be Your name. Your kingdom come. Your will be done on earth as it is in heaven. Give us this day our daily bread. And forgive us our debts, as we forgive our debtors. And do not lead us into temptation, but deliver us from the evil one. For Yours is the kingdom and the power and the glory forever. Amen"* (Matthew 6:9-13). Praying in this manner is a great starting place for us to practice on a regular basis.

Jesus taught us to approach the Father, saying, *"hallowed be Your name."* The word "hallowed" means His name is to be revered or respected. We should open our prayer in this way and then pause—and begin to praise the Father. Give adoration and honor to Him, thanking Him first of all for Who He is and for what He has already given to us in His Son, Jesus Christ.

This time of adoration and praise adjusts our hearts, souls, and minds to see Him in His rightful place and allows us to declare His worth, authority, attributes, and His glory. We should desire to praise God before we petition Him, so spend several minutes thanking and praising the Father for who He is.

Then begin to make the declaration, *"Your Kingdom come, Your will be done on earth as it is in heaven."* Resist the temptation to live as they did in the days of Noah—preoccupied with self rather than God's desires.

Instead, pray on a daily basis for His literal Kingdom to come and that His will would be accomplished on earth, in your personal life, in your spouse's life, in your children's lives (name your children by name), in your extended family, and in your church's life, etc.

Pray for God's will to be made manifest in any person or situation that concerns you. Remember, we are to pray for His will to be done, not ours! We are all tempted to ask God to agree with our plans in life instead of agreeing with His. Our Father does delight in granting our desires, but only if they are in line with His plans for our lives.

Accept His will over yours so as to bring peace to your heart and glory to God. *"'For My thoughts are not your thoughts, Nor are your ways My ways,' says the Lord. 'For as the heavens are higher than the earth, So are My ways higher than your ways, and My thoughts than your thoughts'"* (Isaiah 55:8-9).

Petition Him to literally establish His Kingdom and His will in your life and the lives of those around you. As you faithfully pray for this on a regular basis, accept how He answers your prayer and allow Him to use you for His glory in any and all circumstances.

Next we pray, *"Give us this day our daily bread."* The early church truly depended upon God for their daily food, and so should we. For many of us, God has already provided for today's needs, yet we should pause and thank Him for His provision and continue to ask Him to supply our bread. If there is any excess above what we require, we can give it with joy to others who are hurting, hungry, in need...or who would simply be blessed by receiving it. May we regularly thank Him for meeting our basic needs and for the privilege of giving to others.

Jesus continues teaching us how to pray by stating *"...and forgive us of our debts* (or sins) *as we forgive our debtors* (or those who have sinned against us)."

Yes, forgiveness has already been established in Christ because He is gracious and faithful to pardon us, but we still need to confess our sins and repent (1 John 1:9 and Revelation 2:5). We are also instructed to confess our sins to one another and pray for one another (James 5:16).

We also must forgive others who have sinned against us. Because we have been forgiven, we must forgive, so that anger and bitterness will not be able to penetrate into our hearts. Asking for, and extending forgiveness is liberating and will keep our hearts pure.

Then we continue, *"Do not lead us into temptation, but deliver us from the evil one."* It is important to daily ask the Father to protect us from the enemy and guard our hearts and minds as we put on the armor of God—piece by piece—so we can stand firm in the faith (Ephesians 6:10-18). Since we know we will be tempted by Satan to sin against God, we must ask the Lord to empower us to live lives of holiness.

Finally, we conclude our prayer with a declaration of praise: *"For Yours is the kingdom and the power and the glory forever. Amen and Amen!"* Just as we began the prayer with praise, we should also praise Him as we conclude. He is the King who has all the power to change lives. May we continuously give Him glory!

Peace and Reconciliation Begins with You

Jesus reemphasized the importance of forgiveness right after He taught us how to pray. Matthew 6:14-15 says, *"For if you forgive men their trespasses, your heavenly Father will also forgive you. But if you do not forgive men their trespasses, neither will your Father forgive your trespasses."*

Obviously, this is a huge issue for all of us. Asking for and extending forgiveness keeps our intimacy pure with the Lord and our relationships with others unhindered.

The Apostle Paul wrote, *"If it is possible, as much as depends on you, live peaceably with all men"* (Romans 12:18). How significant this admonition is—under our own roof, with our extended families, our brothers and sisters in Christ, our neighbors, co-workers and community contacts. And how gracious of Paul to say, *"as much as it depends on you."*

We are not called to force people into compliance with us or brow-beat them into a relationship with us! We are called to be peace-loving people, asking forgiveness of one another and extending forgiveness on a regular basis *as much as it depends on us.*

In Scripture we are told: *"Pursue peace with all people, and holiness, without which no one will see the Lord: looking carefully lest anyone fall short of the grace of God; lest any root of bitterness springing up cause trouble, and by this many become defiled"* (Hebrews 12:14-15).

The harsh consequences of *not* living in peace—and living in bitterness—have caused many homes and relationships in

80

and outside the church to deteriorate. Pursuing peace and holiness will bless our households, churches, and communities in ways that will provide a much better atmosphere for love to flourish.

We must remember that there are no flawless churches, flawless marriages, flawless families, or flawless people. One of the reasons that conflict is a part of our lives is that we have not yet been made sinless. In heaven, conflict will not exist because we will not have to contend with our flesh or the enemy tempting us to sin. Until we get to heaven, we will indeed face potential conflict regularly within our relationships.

Jesus knew this would be challenging and He gave us clear instructions on how to handle offenses and pursue peace. These principles apply to all relationships.

If we would practice the following three essential teachings from Jesus we could eliminate bitterness and keep ourselves peaceful and pure, and our witness strong:

First: Overlook the offense!

Jesus taught His disciples to pray, *"And forgive us our debts, As we forgive our debtors. And do not lead us into temptation, but deliver us from the evil one."*

If you can forgive, overlook, and not be tempted with the offense...then simply let it go and move forward. This is an awesome and freeing option. Not being easily offended keeps us free from anger and bitterness. If you are not able to overlook the offense, please follow the teaching of Jesus by embracing one of the next two options (so that you will not be tempted to sin with bitterness).

81

Second: Approach the person who offended you.

Go to the offending individual privately. Receive and give clarification, understanding and/or forgiveness from the other person. If you achieve resolution, you have retained a relationship that would have been damaged or lost, and it keeps you free from bitterness yourself. Press into these conflicts until you have peace, even if there is an agreement to disagree on some issues. If there is no resolution or reconciliation, agree to bring in another person or two as witnesses. If this is not successful, bring the situation to leaders in the church to resolve (Matthew 18:15-20). Don't retreat from the conflict. Press in...<u>until there is peace within you!</u>

Third: Approach those whom you have offended

(real or perceived).

You should immediately go to the person who has expressed that you offended or hurt them. Biblically, the offended individual should come to you first. Typically, that is not what happens. Even if you hear of the offense through someone else, run to the offended person quickly.

It doesn't matter if you agree with their claim, or how they handled the situation. It is real to them and could tempt them to sin with bitterness if not dealt with.

After you address their offense, if how they handled the situation offended you, then deal with that biblically. Again, the goal is to get and receive clarification, understanding, and/or ask for forgiveness. To protect the name of Christ, your integrity, your relationship with this person and so as not to hinder their worship (or yours)...*run* to the offended person at once! (Matthew 5:23-24).

May we experience His peace as we pursue peace with all people, starting with those within our immediate and extended family and the church family,

With all the strife in our homes and in the church, no wonder the discipleship process is hindered. We are called to be reconcilers! I pray we heed our Lord's instructions on how to achieve and live in peace with all people...in as much as it depends upon us. We are not responsible for the response or actions of those with whom we are pursuing peace. We are responsible for our own responses and actions. Jesus said, *"Blessed are the peacemakers, for they shall be called sons of God"* (Matthew 5:9).

PRAYER—IN SUMMARY

The goals of intimacy with our Lord and unhindered relationships with others should keep us in the place of prayer. The Lord has given us a beautiful pattern for praying. Spend time in communicating with Him—not just *to* Him, but *with* Him—as you pause and sit in silence, listening to what He may be saying to you.

Remember, the thoughts that enter your mind may very well be the Lord speaking, even though you may think they originated with you. This is why it is so necessary to be still and ask the Lord to give you spiritual ears to hear what He has to say.

"Be anxious for nothing, but in everything by <u>prayer and supplication, with thanksgiving, let your requests be made</u>

<u>known to God</u>; and the peace of God, which surpasses all understanding, will guard your hearts and minds through Christ Jesus" (Philippians 4:6-7).

There are many things we face in life that cause us concern, anxiety, or uncertainty. Our heavenly Father has given us direct access to Himself through His Son—to hear and to act on our behalf. He instructs us to make our requests known to Him through prayer with thanksgiving.

No matter what we face in life, there is always something to be thankful for. <u>By praying, He assures us that His peace will guard our hearts and minds in Christ. We all need the peace of God during our journey on earth. We obtain it through prayer and by accepting what He does or does not do in our lives</u>.

Take every burden, concern and decision to God through prayer. Then rest and respond as He speaks to your heart. As we are physically in this place of quiet, the Lord will divinely strengthen us. It will also position us to pray without ceasing (Colossians 4:2; 1 Thessalonians 5:17)— simply communicating with God throughout the day; thanking Him for particular blessings, asking for wisdom about a decision, discernment about a relationship or petitioning Him with a specific need, and always...listening for His voice.

May we all find a quiet place...and pray! This precious time with Him will position us to spend the rest of our day in an attitude of continuous prayer.

2. THE WORD

But He answered and said, "It is written,
'Man shall not live by bread alone, but by every
word that proceeds from the mouth of God.'"
– Matthew 4:4

The second spiritual discipline in this first foundation is the written Word of God. Jesus declared, *"If you abide in My word, you are My disciples indeed"* (John 8:31).

The word "abide" means to continue or to remain. Certainly, if we are going to make it our aim to please God, then we need to continue in His Scriptures. In fact, the Word is to dwell inside us in a rich and deep way (Colossians 3:16).

Can we really declare that we are His disciples if we don't desire to read or know His Word? We cannot live out our Christianity based on our pastor's sermon once a week. Just as we need physical food, we desperately need spiritual nourishment as well. <u>We must feed ourselves the Word of God on a daily basis</u>.

This has been a challenge in churches for a long time. You may have heard the following statement characterizing the church in America, "It is a mile wide and an inch deep." When our spiritual roots are not deep or mature, it doesn't take a big test nor the cares and pleasures of this life to knock us over...or out!

Jesus addressed this in the parable of the sower in Luke 8:13-14: *"Those on the rock are the ones who receive the word with joy when they hear it, but they have **no root**. They*

85

*believe for a while, but <u>in the time of testing they fall away</u>. The seed that fell among thorns stands for those who hear, but as they go on their way they are <u>choked by life's worries, riches and pleasures</u>, and they do **not mature.** "*

Notice the words "no root" in verse 13 and the words "not mature" in verse 14—and the consequences that surrounded them. We must mature in our faith.

Scripture tells us: *"Moreover, brethren, I declare to you the gospel which I preached to you, which also you received and in which you stand, by which also you are saved, <u>if you hold fast that word which I preached to you</u>—unless you believed in vain"* (1 Corinthians 15:1-2).

We must feed ourselves daily upon the living Word of God which will cause our spiritual roots to grow deep and strong around our Lord, the Rock of our salvation.

When (not if) the storms of life come upon you, if you follow our Lord's words, your spiritual "house" will stand. *"Therefore whoever <u>hears</u> these sayings of Mine, and <u>does</u> them, I will liken him to a wise man who built his house on the rock: and the rain descended, the floods came, and the winds blew and beat on that house; and it did not fall, for it was founded on the rock. But everyone who <u>hears</u> these sayings of Mine, and <u>does not</u> do them, will be like a foolish man who built his house on the sand: and the rain descended, the floods came, and the winds blew and beat on that house; and it fell. And great was its fall"* (Matthew 7:24-27).

There are blessings for obeying the Word and consequences for disobeying. We will give an account to God for how we viewed and followed His Word. *"Let us therefore* *be diligent to enter that rest, lest anyone fall according to the same example of disobedience. <u>For the word of God is living and powerful</u>, and sharper than any two-edged sword, piercing even to the division of soul and spirit, and of joints and marrow, and is a discerner of the thoughts and intents of the heart. <u>And there is no creature hidden from His sight, but all things are naked and open to the eyes of Him to whom we must give account</u>"* (Hebrews 4:11-13).

THE WORD IS PROFITABLE

"All Scripture is given by inspiration of God, and is <u>profitable</u> for doctrine, for reproof, for correction, for instruction in righteousness, that the man of God may be complete, thoroughly equipped for every good work" (2 Timothy 3:16-17).

I have underscored the word "profitable" because many people in our society view the Word of God as being a set of rules and regulations that restrict life, instead of truth that brings life.

Think about it—everyone likes to profit. Have we come to the point where we view the Word of God as something the Lord has given for our profit? Scripture was written to benefit, help, encourage, and free us. It profits us in our doctrinal insights, which leads us to understanding the heart of God.

His Word corrects, or even rebukes us when our human reasoning and understanding conflicts with His. If applied, the Word will indeed profit us with maturity and will equip us for every good work.

87

The Word of God will not come back void (Isaiah 55:11). It gives us wisdom, guidance, and instruction on how to be fruitful and pleasing to Him. When the Word dwells in us, we will be equipped for the work the Lord has for us and we will worship Him with thankfulness in our hearts (Colossians 3:16-17).

Many feel inadequate or even intimidated to read their Bibles. They believe they're not spiritual enough or they haven't been trained to understand the Scriptures. Others depend only on their pastors or gifted teachers to feed (or teach) them. We thank God for gifted teachers, but God has given every believer the greatest Helper and Teacher of all...and He lives inside us! The Holy Spirit is our live-in resident Teacher and He is available twenty-four hours a day to lead us into all truth (John 14:26; 1 John 2:26-27).

We enjoy the privilege of having at our disposal Bible commentaries, Bible dictionaries, sermons, etc. (and we should use them all) yet, none are as powerful or as accurate as the Holy Spirit. I encourage you to get into your quiet place and read the Word of God systematically, chapter by chapter, asking the Holy Spirit to reveal truth, understanding and righteousness deep into your heart.

The shepherds of God are called to feed the sheep (the Church) and we prayerfully will continue to do so, but the sheep must also feed themselves on His Word or we will not experience the maturity necessary to bear good fruit or to make disciples of our neighbors and all nations.

Don't make your quiet time with God complicated or turn it into another program. He desires for His sons and daughters to return to the quiet place to be alone with Him, to pray, to read His Scriptures, and to worship Him. The Holy Spirit is ready to teach and mature us!

INSTRUCTION AND WISDOM

Reading and applying God's Word to our daily walk will equip us for the work the Lord has called us to do.

When you consider the restrictions of other countries, it is wonderful that we have such an abundance of Bibles in America. Many of us own not just one, but possibly two, three, four, even more.

The question is: are we reading the Bibles we have? Do we cherish the words of life, the sacred Scriptures, and are we receiving instruction and wisdom from them? Through the Word, He speaks to the deep places of our hearts and gives us nourishment.

The nineteenth century minister and author, E. M. Bounds, expresses it beautifully:

Here, let it be said, that <u>no two things are more essential to a Spirit-filled life than Bible reading and secret prayer</u>; no two things more helpful to growth in grace; to getting the largest joy out of a Christian life; toward establishing one in the ways of eternal peace. The neglect of these all-important duties presages leanness of soul, loss of joy, absence of peace, dryness of spirit, decay in all that pertains to spiritual life. Neglecting these things paves the way for apostasy, and gives the evil one an advantage such as he is not likely to ignore. Reading God's Word regularly and *praying habitually in the secret place of the Most High puts one where he is absolutely safe from the attacks of the enemy of souls and guarantees him salvation and final victory through the overcoming power of the Lamb.*

There are few things of greater value that we could do for another person than to teach them how to pray and read their Bible in the quiet place. Just these two aspects alone would change the church if we truly practiced these spiritual disciplines with a passion.

So as not to become legalistic, I'm not suggesting when, or even how much time we should spend in the Word and prayer. I *am* stating that being in the Word and prayer in a quiet place (whether it is morning, noon or night) needs to become an integral part of our *lifestyle* as Christians. If not, we need to stop whatever else we're doing and make sure that these two priorities are incorporated into our lives first, before anything else—period! As the Holy Spirit leads us in prayer and Bible reading, may our spiritual appetite for our Lord continue to increase.

3. PERSONAL WORSHIP

But the hour is coming, and now is, when the true worshipers will worship the Father in spirit and truth; for the Father is seeking such to worship Him. God is Spirit, and those who worship Him must worship in spirit and truth.
– John 4:23-24

The third spiritual discipline of this first foundation on living in relationship with Christ is that of worship.

The question we need to ask ourselves is: As the Father seeks for true worshipers, are we going to be found in that number? To be included, our hearts must reflect thankfulness and gratitude toward God.

Biblical worship is about value. It is our grateful response to what we truly treasure. What we value most determines our actions and becomes the driving force of our lives.

Our worship pastor found and has adopted a beautiful definition of worship when he said, "Worship is our response to God's revelation of Himself."

When Jesus addressed the Pharisees, He said that they honored Him with their lips, <u>but their heart was far from Him</u> (Mark 7:6).

Christianity is not just a set of beliefs. It is a <u>genuine heart</u> relationship with God. We certainly have beliefs that are anchored in the Bible, but they must penetrate our hearts and lead us to the heart of our Lord. When they do, we are able to worship Him freely from the very depths of our being.

Today, the Father is seeking those who are filled with Him and thankful for what He has accomplished for them (Colossians 1:16; Hebrews 13:15-16).

It wasn't just singing or praying that God was looking for as an aspect of worship. It was their very lifestyle. The Pharisees had begun to place the traditions of men before God.

This is still happening today. We can be religious, blindly going through the motions, but the Almighty knows the true condition of our hearts. May our lives reflect our love for Him.

A Living Sacrifice

Scripture teaches through the Apostle Paul, *"Therefore, I urge you, brothers, in view of God's mercy, to offer your bodies as living sacrifices, holy and pleasing to God—this is your spiritual act of worship. Do not conform any longer to the pattern of this world, but be transformed by the renewing of your mind. Then you will be able to test and approve what God's will is—his good, pleasing and perfect will"* (Romans 12:1-2 NIV). Making certain these verses are alive in our bodies, hearts, and minds every day is worship unto God.

Paul also reaffirmed this in Colossians 3:17 when he said, *"Whatever you do in word or in deed, do all in the name of the Lord Jesus, giving thanks to God the Father through Him."*

As we live our lives as holy living sacrifices before God, He receives our lifestyles as continuous worship unto Him. How we love, speak, behave, give, and serve God and others from the heart reveals our depth of worship unto Him.

As we are filled with His presence and our actions prove that He saved us, we will praise His Name from our hearts and sing unto Him. As we worship God with our lifestyles we also worship Him both privately and publically through singing and our physical expressions as well:

- *"Oh come, let us sing to the Lord! Let us shout joyfully to the Rock of our salvation. Let us come before His presence with thanksgiving; Let us shout joyfully to Him with psalms. For the Lord is the great*

God, And the great King above all gods...Oh come, let us <u>worship and bow down</u>; Let us <u>kneel</u> before the Lord our Maker. For He is our God, And we are the people of His pasture, And the sheep of His hand" (Psalm 95:1-3, 6-7).

- *"Make a joyful <u>shout</u> to the Lord, all you lands! Serve the Lord with gladness; Come before His presence with <u>singing</u>"* (Psalm 100:1-2).

- *"I will bless the Lord at all times; His <u>praise</u> shall continually be in my mouth"* (Psalm 34:1).

- *"Behold, bless the Lord, all you servants of the Lord, who by night stand in the house of the Lord. <u>Lift up your hands</u> in the sanctuary, and <u>bless</u> the Lord"* (Psalm 134:1-2).

- *"Oh, <u>clap your hands</u>, all you peoples! <u>Shout</u> to God with the voice of triumph! For the Lord Most High is awesome; He is a great King over all the earth"* (Psalm 47:1-2).

- *"And Ezra blessed the Lord, the great God. Then all the people answered, "Amen, Amen!" while <u>lifting up their hands</u>. And they <u>bowed their heads and worshiped the Lord</u> with their faces to the ground"* (Nehemiah 8:6).

- *"Praise the Lord! <u>Sing</u> to the Lord a new song, and His praise in the assembly of saints. Let Israel rejoice in their Maker; Let the children of Zion be joyful in their King. Let them <u>praise</u> His name <u>with the dance</u>; Let them <u>sing</u> praises to Him <u>with the timbrel and harp</u>. For the Lord takes pleasure in His people; He will beautify the humble with salvation"* (Psalm 149:1-4).

- *"Let everything that has breath, <u>praise</u> the Lord"* (Psalm 150:6).

- *"Speaking to one another in psalms and hymns and spiritual songs, <u>singing</u> and <u>making melody</u> in your heart to the Lord"* (Ephesians 5:19).

- *"Let the word of Christ dwell in you richly in all wisdom, teaching and admonishing one another in psalms and hymns and spiritual songs, <u>singing</u> with grace in your hearts to the Lord"* (Colossians 3:16).

The Bible gives us a picture of David being uninhibited as he praised the Lord. He danced, shouted, gave an offering, blessed the people, and played music (2 Samuel 6:14-22). These are all aspects of worship that we should also recognize and embrace in our personal lives.

David worshiped God with passion even though his own wife (and possibly other people) thought he embarrassed himself and her. He stated to her that he would become even more undignified to show his joy to the Lord.

Our worship of God requires humility, in which our pride falls and we surrender all we are and have, for who He is and for what He has done for us. He has set us free from sin and pride. <u>Only with humility can true worship take place</u>.

May we all humble ourselves before our Lord in gratitude and may the freedom we have in Christ be expressed through us as we declare God's worth in our daily worship of Him!

Certainly as we come together corporately, we lift our hearts and hands to worship Him. It also blesses the heart of our Lord when we, as His sons and daughters, privately worship Him. Again, not only in singing from our hearts, but in using our bodies as living sacrifices, expressions of worship in words, in our actions, in our behavior, and in our giving—all of these are part of our worship.

In addition, how we love and treat our fellow men are reflections of our worship of the One Who saved our souls.

Worship can also be accomplished through singing or just hearing a worship song and letting the words permeate your spirit as you declare God's glory. Reading a psalm and praising God verbally is an act of worship. It declares His worth and can express our reverence, intense love, adoration, honor, and extreme devotion to Him.

SUMMARY OF FOUNDATION 1:
LIVING IN LOVE AND SERVICE TO CHRIST

To practice the spiritual disciplines of *Prayer,* the *Word,* and *Personal Worship,* you begin by finding a quiet place to spend time with the Lord. Don't make it a religious routine or something just to check off your "to-do" list. Be creative with your quiet time to prevent it from becoming legalistic.

As you begin to pray the Lord's Prayer, "My Father Who is in heaven, hallowed be Your name," pause to worship Him for a few moments, blessing and thanking Him, whether it's worship through singing or just simply ascribing to Him His worth. Let everything flow from your heart.

Yes, there are days when you are going to feel more of an attraction to the quiet place than others. Sometimes you just need to be obedient, but don't be overly rigid about it! If you miss a day or two, don't walk around in condemnation. Our goal is to make this a pattern of our lifestyle, something we *desire* to do, that we *need* to do because we *want* to —because it breathes life into our souls and blesses the heart of God.

It is in the place of solitude in the presence of the Lord where our lives, attitudes, and actions are brought into alignment with His.

If we could duplicate and pass on just one aspect of the Christian life to another person, it would be to experience the Lord's presence in a quiet place through listening, praying, reading His Word, and worshiping Him. This one spiritual discipline and privilege would significantly help to keep our hearts pure and purposeful. The Lord could establish and maintain godly homes and churches through us and He would empower us to accomplish the Great Commission.

There is no greater call than our first ministry which is to be given unto our Lord. This will truly bless His heart, and ours!

"HE WAS SPEAKING TO ME"

Let me share this story from a person who has become immersed in the first foundation of Living on Target:

After being a Christian for more than fourteen years, I had never been challenged to go deeper in my relationship with the Lord. I had accepted Him as my Savior and was left right there. I knew it must be important to read the Bible because everyone talked about doing it...but I had no one in my life to whom I was accountable. I read the Bible at times. I prayed each day and I loved singing, but it was really something I did methodically. I felt I needed to do it to be a good little Christian. Unfortunately I became a Christian who lived by a "check-the-box" relationship with the Lord.

Then I was asked to begin Living on Target. I can honestly say that it changed my life! It brought me out of the religious relationship with Christ, into a deep, personal, real relationship with Him. I was asked the hard questions of where I was in the Word, what I was learning and how He was speaking to me. I was asked about my prayer time and my quiet time with the Lord. I had never thought about having a quiet time because quite honestly, my life was anything but quiet.

I came to an understanding about my Heavenly

97

Father and realized that He wanted a real relationship with me and that it was quite personal for Him. Once I understood how He pursued me, loved, me, wanted and longed for that time with me, He became more than a Savior. He became my Lord of all.

I praise God when I receive reports like this!

This first foundation of Living in Love and Service to Christ is the most important of all because every other choice we make will be based on this. Find Him daily in your quiet place. He is your only hope and source of life.

REFLECT AND RESPOND

- Do you really believe God desires to be *with you* before He wants your service? If you do, how are you making sure this is happening?

- Do you have a quiet place to meet God (Matthew 6:6)? If not, where will you choose to get alone with the Lord regularly?

- How would you describe your love for God and your relationship with Him?

- Will you consider using the Lord's Prayer as a model for praying to your Heavenly Father?

- Is receiving and extending forgiveness part of your lifestyle? If not, what steps will you take toward forgiveness?

- If you are not practicing a systematic reading of God's Word, would you begin to read a portion of Scripture each day and ask God to enable you to apply it to your life? What is your plan to make this a reality?

- Will you begin to worship God daily? If this is already a part of your lifestyle, list the ways you find most effective to worship Him.

An abiding relationship with our Lord is the heart of everything else in life.

FOUR

FOUNDATION #2

LIVING IN LOVE AND SERVICE IN THE HOME

Unless the Lord builds the house,
they labor in vain who build it.
— PSALM 127:1

The people who should benefit first and the most from our intimacy with Christ should be our families. God established the home to be a picture of His heart toward us. It should be a place of order and grace, laughter and wholesomeness, vulnerability and discipline, warmth and love.

When we live as true disciples of Christ, we bring to our family members the Lord's example of love and submission to the Father, compassion and servanthood to those around us, transparency and passion for our Father's glory, and joy in the journey.

Sadly, these characteristics often do not typify our homes,

which instead can be filled with shattered dreams, unmet expectations, and broken relationships. Some are filled with anger, silence and even various forms of abuse. Many of our marriages seem to be lukewarm or even in deep trouble. Children often breaking parents' hearts and parents breaking theirs—it is far too common.

Perhaps, other than our relationship with Christ, our home is the area in our life that the enemy is most active in attempting to destroy. This is because our homes are so vital to God's work in the world today. If they are out of biblical order, it hinders our family relationships, our witness, the effectiveness of the Church, and the advancement of the Kingdom.

Next to our relationship with God, our homes are the most important foundation for which we need to achieve and maintain biblical order.

BUILDING STRONG HOMES

Never give up! God knows every detail of your personal life and of your home. He is a God of restoration! Don't run away from God...run *to* Him. Don't run away from your family relationships...run *to* them.

We know that we can't change the past, but repentance and forgiveness can bring healing and restoration to us. Regardless of our family dynamics today, we have the privilege and responsibility to pursue those in our home with peace. Remember, following God's order brings us personal peace and freedom regardless of the responses or actions of our family members.

God has given us very clear instructions in His Word

regarding how our households should function, which is foundational to how the Church should function. In the New Testament, Paul gave Titus a specific strategy for creating a discipling process that would continuously build the lives of the men and women in the church. He knew that having a strong, biblical Church meant having strong, biblical homes.

In Titus 2:1-6, Paul said, *"But as for you, speak the things which are proper for sound doctrine: that the <u>older men</u> be sober, reverent, temperate, sound in faith, in love, in patience; the <u>older women</u> likewise, that they be reverent in behavior, not slanderers, not given to much wine, teachers of good things—that they admonish the young women to love their husbands, to love their children, to be discreet, chaste, homemakers, good, obedient to their own husbands, that the word of God may not be blasphemed."*

Paul looked for the older, mature people in the church to instruct the younger in specific areas of their lives. Are we following this pattern today? We absolutely need more "spiritual fathers and mothers" in the Church to disciple and mentor the younger believers. Their experience and wisdom can bring great benefit to the young men and women of the Faith.

After we help our young people establish intimacy with God, we must teach and model godly characteristics for them regarding the family. If not, they may acquire Bible knowledge but their homes may be out of order. Are we not already experiencing this in great measure today?

MAKING A DIFFERENCE

Whatever the arrangement of our present family

structure—whether we are married...living with our spouse and children, or we are a widow or single adult, if we are a college student, single parent, a couple with no children, or a grandparent with grown children—the biblical principles of God's Word hold true and are applicable today. Regardless of your past, let's restore the biblical order, roles, responsibilities, and joy...<u>one life and home at a time!</u>

We must be filled with hope! The Lord has called us all to live in close and healthy relationship with Him, and to see this duplicated in our homes. He not only calls us, but empowers us!

Today, you can start the process of making a difference. You can begin to establish the order, joy and peace God intended from the beginning. No home is perfect, but it can be a dwelling where we are growing and learning to live by God's Word.

Next, we will address the aspects of men and women and their roles and responsibilities in the family, and how finances should be handled. All three of these areas must be put in order, not only for our own sanity and peacefulness, but for the advancement of the Kingdom and so that we will be found pleasing to our Lord.

1. SINGLE

The Apostle Paul, in 1 Corinthians 7:6-9, 24-35, speaks to singles regarding their singleness. If they were single at the time 1 Corinthians was written, Paul encouraged them to stay single (as he was) in order to give all of their time and attention to pleasing the Lord and advancing the Kingdom. He stated that time was short and stressful and that they were to live their lives as if this present world were passing away.

These verses can be difficult to accept, especially if there is a strong yearning to be married (and certainly Paul is not against that). He is just emphasizing the opportunity to *"serve the Lord without distraction."* Certainly, these principles are applicable to us today.

When you are married with children, your family needs to be given priority. It takes time and effort to invest into a family. If you are unmarried, then you are free to use your days to serve God without the responsibilities of marriage and children.

I certainly realize, through Scripture and life in general, that inside of most people God has placed a longing and a desire to be married. The Lord does, indeed, give some a gift to remain single all of their life that they may use their singleness to advance the Kingdom.

If you are an individual to whom God has given this assignment, then praise the Lord! Continue to be used for His glory and dedicate your life to serve the Church and help to fulfill the Great Commission. May God bless and use you in a very powerful way!

If you feel God has not given you the assignment of singleness and you have a desire to be married, remember while you are single, to use your gifts, talents, time, and everything that is at your disposal for the advancement of His Kingdom. If you become too occupied with finding a mate, you may find yourself being continually dissatisfied and ineffective with the treasure of days you were given.

Enjoy your life and the relationships that God brings to you. Use your gifts and talents to serve our Lord. Please consider discipling children, teenagers, and any other people of your gender that God may call you to. Single parents often need godly men and women to assist them with their children and there will always be evangelistic and missions opportunities to participate in.

Keep yourself occupied with our Lord and His mission... which will empower you to stay strong in faith and purity. When, (not if) you experience the temptation of immorality, *"Submit to God. Resist the devil and he will flee from you"* (James 4:7).

Remember, you must honor your "brothers" and "sisters" with sexual purity, guarding your heart from all impurity (1 Thessalonians 4:1-8). For sexual (or any) temptation (including pornography), God has provided a way of escape. *"No temptation has overtaken you except such as is common to man; but God is faithful, who will not allow you to be tempted beyond what you are able, but with the temptation will also make the way of escape, that you may be able to bear it"* (1 Corinthians 10:13). He will give you the power to control your body. And you are called to live in relational responsibility and transparency with others who share your heart for purity.

The Lord knows the longing of your heart. While I don't pretend to perceive the exact will of God for any person, I do know from Scripture that whatever condition we are in, we are to live our lives in contentment. This doesn't mean we don't have dreams and desires that we lay before Him...but we are instructed to be content in all things and to be used by the Lord while we wait for our heart's longings to be fulfilled in Him.

Those who are single must put their homes and relation-ships in biblical order just like any other family. This objective should be sought in extended family relationships and with any others who may live with you.

The call is the same for you as it is for those who are married...<u>be</u> and <u>make</u> disciples! May our Lord Jesus raise up multitudes of men and women like Himself; single, but not alone, united with His Father and empowered by the Holy Spirit to change the world. Go for it!

2. MARRIED

*And the LORD God said, "It is not good that
man should be alone; I will make him a helper
comparable to him." And the LORD God caused
a deep sleep to fall on Adam, and he slept; and He
took one of his ribs, and closed up the flesh in its place.
Then the rib which the LORD God had taken from man
He made into a woman, and He brought her to the man.
And Adam said: "This is now bone of my bones and
flesh of my flesh; She shall be called Woman, because
she was taken out of Man." Therefore a man shall
leave his father and mother and be joined to
his wife, and they shall become one flesh.*
–GENESIS 2:18, 21-24

Marriage...God's Way

God made man. God made woman out of him and for him. The man is to leave his father and mother and join to his wife and they shall become one. We need to leave any worldly definitions of marriage and family behind and cleave to the truths of God's Word.

When we share the *biblical* concept of marriage and the roles and responsibilities of husbands and wives in modern society, people often think that it is old fashioned or outdated. God's standards are not defined by society, and society's definitions of roles within the home are obviously not working.

We don't need any new definitions of marriage and family. As a result of this attempt, gender and marriage confusion is very prevalent in our society. This is causing tremendous pain, unfulfillment, fornication, adultery, divorce, and confusion. God is not the author of confusion. He and His Word are clear on these subjects. The Church must echo the absolute truth of Scripture in a culture of relative truth. We will only experience freedom and fulfillment when we function as we were created to function within our marriages and homes. Many Christian families can testify to this.

In His image, God made male and female equal, but different. There is absolutely no difference in value (Genesis 1:26-27), only in function. We should celebrate the differences and fulfill our roles and responsibilities before God, our spouses, and our children. We will be blessed. Our families will be blessed...and God will be blessed.

We will not be able to instruct our young men or young women in what a godly man or woman is—or how they are to function—if we don't believe what God's Word says regarding who we are and how we are to live out our lives.

May we as men and women truly value what the Word says about us and fulfill our unique purposes before God and our families with passion and conviction.

One of the greatest gifts we can give our children and grandchildren is the example of a godly marriage. If this is not your experience right now, please know that God's Word will bring you peace...and position you to develop a godly and joyful partnership.

Marriage is being attacked on every side. In fact, society is attempting to redefine this union which was established by God. Since the beginning, marriage was always intended to be between one man and one woman. In God's eyes, it always will be!

There is a distinction between male and female. God designed us to function uniquely and differently. He has given men certain assignments—just as He has given for women. Sadly, in our culture we are attempting to either blur those lines or to obliterate them completely and create some unisex person who simply does not exist.

The distinctiveness and order of God's creation is emphasized again for us in 1 Corinthians 11:3, Ephesians 6:1-3, and Colossians 3:18-21. Christ is the head of every man, the man is the head of the wife, the husband and wife are the head or the leaders of the children, and thus there is order and distinctiveness in the family.

For fathers to properly raise their sons to be men, we need to know and practice what God has called men to be. The same is true for women.

ROLES AND RESPONSIBILITIES OF HUSBANDS AND WIVES

In my experience as a pastor, one of the biggest obstacles

for marriages to experience peace and freedom is the lack of understanding or lack of desire to understand and practice the distinct biblical roles and responsibilities of husbands and wives. This is causing tremendous hurt in our homes and it will tempt our children to look to our present culture (instead of mom and dad) to define marriage.

The presence of godly men, not only in our homes, but also in our churches and communities, is essential, and the world will see the benefits. However, before the world experiences the worth of godly men, our wives and children should benefit first! The absence of such men, husbands, and fathers seems to wreak havoc, and we are seeing tremendous consequences as a result. Men, rise up and fulfill your role. Our families, churches and society need you.

In the context of marriage, the husband is to submit to the Lord first. His <u>role</u> as the head of his wife, is to lead her spiritually, emotionally and physically. *"For the husband is head of the wife…"*(Ephesians 5:23. See also 1 Corinthians 11:3). His <u>responsibility</u> is to love his wife as Christ loved the Church (Ephesians 5:25-33 and Colossians 3:19). This is a tremendous amount of love that is impossible to give unless God's love is flowing through him.

A husband is also to financially provide for his family (1 Timothy 5:8 and 2 Thessalonians 3:10), possibly with his wife's help if necessary…but not to the neglect of his personal involvement with his family. Men can live in the home, but still be absent emotionally.

If your young children don't live with you, take care of them financially and spend as much time with them as possible. Men, we <u>cannot abandon</u> our wives and children spiritually, emotionally, physically or financially. Remember, we will give an account before God!

There is protection and fulfillment for our wives and our children under our spiritual covering when we are submitting to the Lord.

Here's what a leader in our church shared:

The Living on Target process has established in me a consistency of being in His presence and abiding in His Word on a daily basis that I had never previously experienced. It has also created in me a profound challenge of loving my wife as Christ loves His church! The simplicity and yet profoundness of this discipleship process has had a powerful impact on my life. If it were possible to take an x-ray of my inner man, I believe anybody would be able to see those "crosshairs" of the Target etched into my heart and mind!

In order to live the life God desires, men must assume their rightful place in the home. They must do so with humility and submission, yet with clarity, passion, and with conviction to lead their wives and children in a manner that is pleasing to the Lord.

It is my prayer that the Almighty raises up an army of godly men who will not retreat from their families, but who will run toward them. May we witness many men who take their rightful position in the home and church, who will leave legacies for their sons and daughters; godly husbands and fathers who are not ashamed of Jesus.

I long to see husbands and fathers who are not embarrassed to show affection to their wives, sons, and daughters—to say the words "I love you," to physically touch, hug, and kiss them, to read and model Scripture and truly be an example of what a godly man is all about. What a legacy for our wives and children to follow...as they observe us loving Christ, them, and the mission of the church. May we see this take place, for the sake of our wives, children, grandchildren, church and society—all for the glory of God!

Godly women, no one can take your place. No one! We need you. Our families, churches, and society need you. It is essential for godly women to boldly take their rightful place in the home, church and society—women who will not be ashamed of Jesus or His Word, or the work to which He has called them. Society will continue its attempts to redefine what a woman is, how she should look, dress, behave, and how she should parent. But Scripture must be our guide, not culture, not magazines—but God's Holy Word.

Wives, you have an amazing influence in your homes to draw your husbands into the things of God just by living with them in love, respect, submission, and contentment.

Deep in the heart of every woman is a desire to be loved deeply, led gently, and spiritually covered by her husband. A godly wife will fulfill her <u>role</u> by helping her husband in whatever he needs. *"And the LORD God said, "It is not good that man should be alone; I will make him a <u>helper comparable</u> to him..."* (Genesis 2:18-24; also see 1 Corinthians 11:3, 8-9, 11-12).

It is a wise man who partners with his wife, asking for her wisdom and insight. He remains the head of the home and the ultimate responsibility rests on his shoulders, but he has a trusted partner with whom he is safe and from whom he *can receive a different perspective. Wives, we need you.*

A wife will fulfill her responsibility to biblically submit and respect by supporting his leadership of the family while providing rich, gentle input and safe partnership. "Wives, submit to your own husbands, as to the Lord. Therefore, just as the church is subject to Christ, so let the wives be to their own husbands in everything" *(Ephesians 5:22, 24; see also Colossians 3:18 and Titus 2:15).*

What an amazing comparison! The Church receives protection and security from Her relationship with Christ. He died for the Church. He loves Her with a sacrificial and joyful love. To submit to Christ is in Her best interest. For a wife to submit to her husband is also in her best interest.

If you happen to be a wife whose husband is not obeying the Word, your natural tendency may be to nag and complain and be fearful, but Scripture teaches us in 1 Peter 3:1-6, "Wives, likewise, be submissive to your own husbands, that even if some do not obey the word, they, without a word, may be won by the conduct of their wives, when they observe your chaste conduct accompanied by fear (respect). *Do not let your adornment be merely outward—arranging the hair, wearing gold, or putting on fine apparel—rather let it be the hidden person of the heart, with the incorruptible beauty of a gentle and quiet spirit, which is very precious in the sight of God. For in this manner, in former times, the holy women who trusted in God also adorned themselves, being submissive to their own husbands, as Sarah obeyed Abraham, calling him lord, whose daughters you are if you do good and are not afraid with any terror."*

Wives, I am not suggesting that you submit in situations when your husband may become violent or when he demands that you sin against God or His Word. Honor him, even if you don't fully agree with him, and attempt to win him through your godly conduct. In these unfortunate situations, you may be tempted to act in the flesh and demand your rights or try to be the Holy Spirit. Instead, resist the thoughts of the enemy and live by the power of the Holy Spirit to react and respond in a godly and loving manner. Your godly conduct will bless the heart of your Lord and the lives of those around you.

When Peter addresses women in 1 Peter 3:4, he encourages them not to rely on external appearance for their value but to adorn themselves in the *"...hidden person of the heart, with the incorruptible beauty of a gentle and quiet spirit, which is very precious in the sight of God."*

Peter wasn't advocating silence in all situations. In this passage he was addressing a woman's spirit. There are godly women of different personality types who all can fit this description. A woman whose heart is calm, who is not harsh, who has (in her spirit) a strong and peaceful center...this is very precious to God, and can only be a reality when the Holy Spirit is in control.

God longs to see older women who mentor younger women in the church: who teach them intentionally how to *"love their husbands, to love their children, to be discreet, chaste, homemakers, good, obedient to their own husbands, that the word of God may not be blasphemed"* (Titus 2:4-5). This mentoring is crucial, especially during difficult times when husbands and children are not acting lovably.

Living on Target was used by God to bring powerful change in a woman's life and in her marriage. She recounted:

I never realized how much God really cared about my marriage and my role as a wife. Although my life was out of order it has been changed and transformed.

The journey started when I approached people in my life who I had given priority over my husband. I repented and asked them to hold me accountable to never put them there again. I did not realize the impact it would make on others, I was just trying to be obedient. My sister was one of the people I put before my husband. When I went to her and repented, she was convicted to do the same in her marriage.

I then went to my husband. Wow, he broke down. Never did I realize that sharing this with him and repenting for putting other people in his place would bring a closeness between us that I did not even realize we both were longing for. This started a journey for us in communicating. It also started a journey of learning to trust each other again. As I started taking steps to walk in my role and letting Christ fill the holes in my heart that were there from the past, then God starting healing my marriage.

I am finally walking in the God-given role and place God designed for me. I am able to love, respect, and encourage my husband. By learning to be the right person for my mate, he has been impacted and is learning to become the right person for me. Now that is God at work! He has totally restored our marriage and I am walking in such a place of freedom and love and respect for my husband, now that I understand God's heart for me as a wife.

Within the holy calling to women is a vast freedom to embrace differing personalities, giftedness, skills, and passions. Don't be limited by the misconception that all godly wives and mothers have the same strengths and methods, and manage their homes identically. Although there are biblical principles that guide them, when women follow God's Word with determination, they will be free to develop their God-given strengths and giftedness to be expressed richly in their homes, their churches, and their communities.

Wives, after your relationship with Christ, your family (husband, children, home) should be your primary priority—even if you have to, or choose to, work outside the home. <u>Your home should be where your heart is</u>. The Proverbs 31 woman seems to be a savvy businesswoman, but it is clear that her home was her priority. As you give precedence to your home, may your children rise up and call you blessed and may your husband praise you! (Proverbs 31:28).

There are obviously different seasons of life that allow for differing allocation of time. Not every woman functions well with the same level of demands. Remember, however, that if a woman's heart leaves her home, <u>devastating results will always be experienced</u>.

Be encouraged! No heart is impossible for God to change.

May you be an absolute blessing to your husband, children, grandchildren, church, and society...all for the glory of God!

How Marriage was Meant to be Lived Out

"Nevertheless let each one of you in particular so <u>love his own wife as himself,</u> and let the wife see <u>that she respects her husband</u>" (Ephesians 5:33). Love from husbands and respect from wives are critical attributes to achieve joyful and secure marriages. A marriage, as it was meant to be lived, works in a <u>mutually-giving cycle.</u>

When a husband loves and submits to the Lord, and loves and leads his wife, it causes his wife to desire to respect him. Her response motivates her husband to love and lead even more, which causes his wife to respect and respond to his leadership even more. You can see where this is going...it is a beautiful cycle. This is how marriage was meant to be lived out!

Even so, life is hard. No one desires to have more discouragement in their life. We all need encouragement. We must tell each other that we appreciate what the other is giving and doing for us and for the family.

We are all human and we will continue to have disagreements and struggles, yet with this ongoing cycle of love and respect being given and received, both husband and wife will breathe life into each other. This is how husbands and wives should function. When we do, marriage is awesome!

It is when one or both spouses begin to live selfishly in the flesh that trouble starts...and it can become very hurtful! If one spouse neglects their role and responsibility, it does not negate the other spouse from theirs. It's bad enough when one partner is living in the flesh, but when they both do—watch out. Heartbreak is at hand!

We are to walk in the Lord and in our marriage function regardless of the action or attitude of our spouse. Our Lord will give us peace and power to live as the witness He has called us to be. God desires to use our love, respect and conduct as He convicts our spouse of sin.

Husbands and wives, are you ready to gently and honestly discuss how you are doing in fulfilling your biblical roles and responsibilities? Without attacking, and with a non-defensive heart, share some insights from each person's perspective.

Husband, are you leading and loving your wife in a way that breathes life into her? Wife, share with your husband the ways you are experiencing his leadership and love. Then communicate the ways that you may feel a lack in these areas and what you desire from him.

Wife, are you helping and biblically respecting (submitting to) your husband in a manner that breathes life into him? Husband, share with your wife the ways you are experiencing that help and respect. Then let her know if you feel a lack in these areas and what you desire from her.

It is imperative that we honor the Lord by following our identity in Him as saints of God, as sons and daughters of the Most High and to function as He has created us to function as husbands and wives. If we do, our marriages and families will be satisfying and our Lord will be glorified.

HONEST QUESTIONS, HONEST ANSWERS

The following dialogue exercise has also proven to be extremely beneficial to couples. Honestly ask your spouse how well you participate in the spiritual, emotional, and physical intimacy of your marriage. Be open concerning what you need to give to your spouse in these areas and then listen to what your mate says he or she desires from you. (Not what you *think* they desire, but what your spouse *knows* they desire.)

Please communicate gently from your heart and receive what your spouse is communicating without becoming defensive or angry. The Scriptures teach us to speak the truth in love (Ephesians 4:15). This type of communication is necessary to establish and maintain joyful and satisfying marriages.

Share truthfully what you require from each other *spiritually* (praying, reading, going to church together), *emotionally* (conversation, affection, time together, laughing, romance), and *physically* (exercising together, physical touch, fulfilling each other's sexual needs). There is no better time than the present! Pursuing your spouse in these three ways helps to resist any immorality that tempts you to draw away from your spouse. Unfortunately, pornography, adultery, on-line relationships, and other forms of fornication are wreaking havoc in our personal and married lives.

The answer Paul gave to the temptation of sexual immorality was that the husband and wife were to meet each other's sexual needs (1 Corinthians 7:1-5). Please understand this...because of immoral sexual temptation, each man should have his own wife and each woman her own husband. What a clear and biblical solution to temptation ...your spouse!

When spiritual, emotional, and physical desires are lovingly met within the marriage, there should be absolutely no excuse to look outside your marriage (including pornography) for satisfaction. Even if desires are not fully met, there is never an excuse to commit adultery...never! *"Therefore, submit to God. Resist the devil and he will flee from you"* (James 4:7).

Under no circumstances should men be talking to women other than their wives (or women to men other than their husbands) about the intimate spiritual, emotional, or physical issues of their marriage (unless with a godly pastor, discipler, or counselor). These conversations can open up an emotional door that must not be opened. Don't do it!

It might be awkward or even painful to know what your spouse is struggling with and what he or she needs from you, but the alternative of a disconnected marriage or an unfaithful spouse will be even more painful. Communicate with God and with your spouse. Do not retreat. Your marriage is worth it!

TWO-WAY COMMUNICATION

Though God has clearly established biblical order, we are also called to mutually submit to one another out of love and honor for each other (Ephesians 5:21-33). Men, we would all benefit by listening to our wives. They have insight and a perspective that we absolutely need. God gave us a helpmate because He knew that we needed help! Prayerfully consider your wife's perspective and wisdom before making crucial decisions. This will draw you closer together, and you will both receive the benefits of your combined wisdom. You are still responsible to lead ...with love and wisdom.

Men, if you are like me, we sometimes think we have an answer before our wives even ask a question. We need to truly listen to our spouses. Sometimes, our wives aren't looking for a solution. Their hearts are simply longing to be heard by their husband.

Scripture teaches us that we are to live with our wives in an understanding way, showing honor to them. This will benefit our wives and it will benefit us. Our prayers will not be hindered (1 Peter 3:7) and we will profit from our wives' perspectives.

Often, the best response to our wives can be repeating what they stated and showing affection (a hug or a gentle kiss, etc.). We don't always need to fully understand, just to believe and trust in the importance of communication and to be there for them, showing how much we deeply care. I am growing in this area myself. I am continually learning from my wonderful wife and daughter about how to be a listener. They are great teachers!

Women, as you desire communication from your husbands, be aware of the various ways they communicate. Don't dismiss an act of service as being unrelated to his love for you. They may not express themselves exactly as you would, so honor them by accepting their forms of communication just as you desire the same from them.

As you talk with your husband and you're being heard, be sure to also listen carefully to his perspective. Allow him to fully express his thoughts. Then, it is extremely important that you honor and respect him in following his leadership in a way that breathes life into him. Even if the final decision is not exactly as you thought it should be, give him the honor of following as a partner and encourager.

Learn which times are best for talking together. Bringing up deep wounds or engaging in intense discussion may not be wise when one or both of you is extra tired. Men and women can both have challenges in communication but as we listen, learn, and respond appropriately to each other, healing and life will be constantly breathed into our marriages. This won't just happen. We have to constantly pursue our spouse with love, respect, and communication in order to achieve and maintain a fulfilling marriage. It is well worth the effort!

COMMITMENT AND LOYALTY

One of the older, spiritually mature men in a group I was leading applied the biblical order principle of sacrificially loving his wife by asking what her true desires were, and then trying various ways to meet them. He was amazed to discover how much their marriage relationship improved!

Once you acknowledge the importance of your desires, remember that no person was created to meet each and every one of them. Only God can ultimately supply what is required.

We are called to be used by God to bless and enrich the lives of our spouses, being His conduit for love and encouragement.

We all know that we have fallen short in our marriage relationship at one time or another. When we hurt our spouse, we must ask for forgiveness from our heart with a true desire to change our behavior. Confessing our sin and praying for one another can bring healing.

May this process of asking for and receiving forgiveness, discussing roles, responsibilities, and sharing desires, hopes and dreams bring healing life and joy into our marriages. This communication process is a large part of us Living on Target for the glory of God. May your marriage be all that you and God desire for it to be!

I have had the joy of being married to my wife and best friend, Amy, for twenty-three years. We have attempted to faithfully (not flawlessly) follow the teachings presented in this chapter. They have brought us peace, joy, fulfillment, contentment and continued love for each other. To God be the glory!

As we Live on Target in our marriages, we are modeling Christianity for our children. May we give our children one of the most valuable gifts of all; a godly marriage for them to gain security from and a model to follow as they prepare for marriage.

Christian Parenting

In the Gospels, we have this wonderful, tender glimpse into Jesus' compassion for children: *"Then little children were brought to Him that He might put His hands on them and pray, but the disciples rebuked them. But Jesus said, 'Let the little children come to Me, and do not forbid them; for of such is the kingdom of heaven'"* (Matthew 19:13-15).

The disciples were probably attempting to protect Jesus' time and energy, yet they missed His love and heart for the children. He had a genuine desire to be with them!

An observation of our family relationships today begs the question: do we as parents have a desire to be with our children and to train them in the ways of our Lord? Do we have a passion to show them affection and care, give them clear spiritual direction, and influence them for God's glory? Or do we regard our children as a distraction and an invasion of our time? Jesus reprimanded His disciples for adopting this attitude!

Whether our children will be subjected to spiritual influences is not in question. The question is—*how* will they be influenced and *who* will impact them the most? Simply put, our Lord has chosen *parents*, and in particular, the *fathers* to be the primary spiritual influence for children. Ephesians 6:4 states, *"And you, fathers, do not provoke your children to wrath, but bring them up in the training and admonition of the Lord."*

Our children, whether they admit it or not, long for a loving and healthy relationship with their fathers. The wounds that many sons or daughters carry from absent (either physically or emotionally) or abusive fathers is so tragic and so unnecessary! May the hearts of the fathers turn back to their children and the hearts of the children to their fathers (Malachi 4:5-6; Luke 1:17).

The importance of godly mothers is indescribable! Our children need involved mothers who teach and care for their children with affection and sacrificial love. A woman who is sincere in her faith and confident in God's call to godly motherhood, will have an eternal impact on her children.

If we, as fathers and mothers, have caused wounds,

intentionally or unintentionally, we must repent and ask our children (in an age appropriate way) for their forgiveness. May healing, restoration and revival begin with us.

Our children are the most precious earthly gift God has given us (Psalm 127:3-5), and we have the privilege and responsibility to love and train them in His ways (Deuteronomy 6:4-9; Ephesians 6:4). The Lord seeks godly offspring (Malachi 2:14-16).

DISCIPLE YOUR CHILDREN RELATIONALLY

Living on Target as a lifestyle with our children is a wonderful way to train and disciple them, but we must establish a trusting relationship first. Please remember, rules and instruction without a relationship usually lead to rebellion.

Our children must know that we love them unconditionally. Tell them and show them! Hug, kiss and affirm them whenever possible and appropriate. Please lovingly correct and discipline your children when necessary to also show your love and concern. Don't be afraid to tell them what they need to hear. Speak the truth in love (Ephesians 4:15). They need you to be their parent.

Find the best way to connect with your child. It has been a joy for me to date my daughter and have "Dad Nights" with my sons. We can just hang out, eat together, shop, watch a ball game or talk about life. I can encourage them in their walk with God and others and help them develop a biblical world view.

Each child is uniquely different. Your approach to your

children may vary …but never give up on connecting with them. It may be sports, video games, exercise, shopping or "coffee" etc. Find out how to connect and do it as often as you can. This opens their heart for other meaningful communication.

Attempt to be a safe place for listening, encouragement, laughter, and having fun together. These things are absolutely necessary to create a loving bond between parent and child (of any age). Don't make discipling your children a purely academic process. Yes, read the Word to them, but also show them the Word in your Living on Target lifestyle.

As you're living life with your children, you will have the connection to walk with them in their struggles, victories, decision-making, friendships, etc.

How we handle life's decisions, how we respond to conflict, and our desire to fulfill the mission of His Church all contribute to the discipling of our children. Though we make mistakes as we raise our sons and daughters, there is forgiveness and hope in Christ! As a matter of fact, even how we handle our shortcomings or mistakes is also a part of the discipling process.

Let us purpose in our hearts to become the parents that He desires for us to be: *our children need and deserve godly parents!*

CHILDLIKE FAITH

Our first step in training our children is to acknowledge Jesus' desire that we become childlike in our faith toward Him. In the words of our Lord, *"Assuredly, I say to you, unless you are converted and become as little children, you will by no means enter the kingdom of heaven"* (Matthew 18:3).

The disciples were arguing over who would be the greatest in the Kingdom of Heaven. Jesus uses little children as examples of humility, dependence, and faith—qualities without which no one would enter the Kingdom.

We all need these same characteristics as we surrender our lives to Christ and continue in relationship with Him—and they are required in parenting.

MISTAKE-FREE PARENTING?

Being a mom or dad can be the most rewarding and, at the same time, one of the most challenging aspects of our life. The pain we feel when our children are sick, sinful, hurting, struggling, in trouble, or rebellious can be overwhelming. We may ask ourselves what we could have done to prevent such problems, or we may make a list of the "should haves."

Certainly, we must evaluate our involvement (or lack of) and take responsibility and correction where necessary...and when we do, we all need the comfort of Christ's love and the compassion of brothers and sisters being poured out on us. "Pat" answers and condemnation are just not acceptable.

There are many godly parents who have loved, taught, and guided their children in a very biblical manner, yet their children still choose not to walk with God. Sometimes it's not the parents' fault, rather it is the decision of the child or teenager. Christian parents who have faithfully tried to train their children up in the way they should go—and are living with shame because their children made, or are making ungodly choices—need to leave that shame at the cross. Be careful not to judge parents too quickly. Remember your own teenage years and the lessons you learned. You may have had (or caused) conflicts with your own parents in the process of growing up.

Parenting takes courage and commitment, and we cannot retreat from our responsibilities. Parents who don't walk with their children through life, who neglect to help develop a biblical world view in their children, and who stick their heads in the sand...need to repent and begin to engage in the spiritual battle for the hearts of their sons and daughters.

If there has not been a safe relationship built, your children will need time to recognize that your instruction and involvement are coming out of love for them and a desire to be obedient to God. You may need to express your repentant heart to them and your desire to begin a new relationship and direction with them.

As parents, we all have made mistakes, and will continue to do so. An expectation of arriving at the perfection of "mistake-free" parenting is bondage and can be idolatry! At the same time, we cannot excuse ourselves from praying for and investing into our children spiritually, both in word and in deed. The principles of God's Word are still in effect and apply today.

If your relationship with your children (no matter what age) is not what you'd like...pursue them! _Even if they don't seem to respond, don't ever give up. Although you mustn't enable your children's sin, you need to love and pray for them unceasingly._

With your older teenage and adult children, participate in their lives to whatever extent they allow. If you know that you have blown it in certain areas with them, ask for forgiveness. Asking for and extending forgiveness is the key to reconciling and restoring any relationship. We will not always be perfect, but we can and should be faithful.

This is why we must come to Christ ourselves in childlike faith, humility, and dependence. Godly wisdom is essential as we lead and guide our sons and daughters, and this is exactly what Christ provides as we remain dependent on Him (1 Corinthians 1:30).

What a relief to know that we don't have to parent in our own strength and wisdom! We have all faced frustration from trying it on our own. Thankfully, the Lord loves each one of our children so much that He desires to care for and parent them "through us" as we stay surrendered to Him. This is great news for every mother and father!

We will still face challenges, but we will also experience the joys and rewards of parenting. We must not quit! We must never give up—on God's power, on ourselves as parents, or on our children. May we raise godly offspring that will rise up and be a blessing to God, to us, to the Church, and to the world.

3. FINANCES

Jesus made this statement: *"No one can serve two masters; for either he will hate the one and love the other, or else he will be loyal to the one and despise the other. You* _cannot serve God and mammon"_ (Matthew 6:24). The word "mammon" is another word for riches or money.

Proper handling of money has become a major obstacle for people and we must either get this part of our life in order and under control or we will be rendered ineffective for the Lord and Christian service. Financial pressure can seem overwhelming and it will test the resolve of even the strongest people and marriages.

Money is a spiritual issue and God knew we would have to deal with it daily. Either we, by the Spirit, will control money, or money will control us. There is no middle ground! God owns everything we have, not just the tithes and offerings. When His mission becomes our mission personally, we will view and use His money with eternity in mind. We are stewards of His resources and will one day give an account of how we used them (Luke 16:11-12). May we use them to properly care for our families and for other Kingdom purposes.

WHERE IS YOUR TREASURE?

In Matthew 6:19-21, Jesus stated that where our treasure is, there would be our heart also. He tells us not to store up for ourselves treasures on earth where moth and rust and thieves can break in and steal, but to store up for ourselves _treasures in heaven._ Wow! Even though we may not know exactly how we will experience this in heaven, it is still what the Bible teaches and we can rejoice in its reality.

A dear man of God in our church who is well along in years shared with me the adventure he and his wife experienced in this area of discipleship. He wrote:

The part of "Living on Target" that impressed my wife and me the most was to determine where our priorities were in life. The question we asked ourselves was: "where are our treasures"?

Our lives have been greatly impacted, especially in the area of finances. Our focus used to be what we had accumulated in "stuff" and we realize now that material things don't really matter in light of eternity. Along with other lifestyle changes, we both felt compelled by the Lord to give a large amount of money from the savings we had been accumulating for our retirement. As we sought the Lord individually as to the amount He wanted us to give, He told each of us separately the exact same amount! We gave with joy, adjusting our lifestyle in order to live as good stewards.

In the past few years, we have kept a list of the blessings that the Lord has poured back into our lives. God has given us amazing benefits. Living by His principles has brought specific blessings and financial soundness but we are also careful to note the non-financial blessings that He has sent. His Kingdom economy looks very different from our earthly economy. We are delighted to invest in eternal things, trusting Him to supply what we truly need.

It's only laying up treasures in Heaven that count because this is how the Gospel can be spread both at home and abroad (Matthew 6:19-21). Every day we thank the Lord that we are privileged to lay up those treasures!

AN ETERNAL FOUNDATION

In 1 Timothy 6:17-19 Paul tells us we are to continue to be generous givers and that as we are giving and sharing what God has blessed us with, we are *laying up for ourselves a good foundation* for the time to come. A literal definition of this concept may be impossible in our finite minds, but this is what the Bible teaches. So as we're giving, we are not only blessing God and being obedient to Him, it also is to our benefit personally that we do so. Somehow, when we reach heaven we are going to be blessed with what we have presented to God on earth. He loves to bless His children and their obedience.

Please understand, we are not giving simply and only to receive—but rather because we have already received. It is a blessing and an honor to give to the Lord. The Father has already favored us with the ultimate gift of eternal life to be with Him forever and ever. This would be enough, but He desires to bless obedience—and we should desire to receive His blessing. What a generous God we serve!

Christians should be characterized as people of extreme generosity because of our extreme thankfulness unto our Lord, and because of our passion to fulfill the mission He has given us.

GODLY CONTENTMENT

Paul said, *"Now godliness with <u>contentment</u> is great gain.*

132

For we brought nothing into this world, and it is certain we can carry nothing out. And having food and clothing, with these we shall be <u>content</u>" (1Timothy 6:6-8).

Notice the words "great gain." The greatest increase we can achieve is a life content in God and His mission. If we truly love and obey Him (godliness) we will live lives of contentment which will bring us great gain.

Author John Piper is quoted as saying, "God is most glorified in us when we are most satisfied in Him."

If and when God's sons and daughters get to this place of satisfaction in Him, can you imagine the impact on our giving? His priority will be reflected in ours. What is important to Him will be important to us. We will begin to see the Church and the world the way He sees it—and His mission will become our mission.

The Scripture also confirms that with food and clothing we shall be content. These items are seen as rights in our country, but they are not rights—they are blessings! God forgive us…we are <u>so</u> blessed!

"Command those who are rich in this present age not to be haughty, nor to trust in uncertain riches but in the living <u>God, who gives us richly all things to enjoy</u>. Let them do good, <u>that they be rich in good works, ready to give, willing to share, storing up for themselves a good foundation for the time to come</u>, that they may lay hold on eternal life" (1Timothy 6:17-19).

Paul commanded those who are rich not to be prideful, but we may have already fallen into this trap. It seems from Scripture that the definition of "rich" is simply having more food and clothing than you need. Evaluate if you are rich or not according to this definition. We certainly have our financial challenges in America and in our homes, but most of us have food and clothing—and even more than we need! May we complain less, be thankful more, and make financial decisions based upon His mission and not just our wants and desires.

FAITH AND FINANCES

Our flesh will never be satisfied…it always wants more! Paul had to learn in Christ how to live a life of contentment as he matured in the faith, and so should we. In Philippians 4:11-13 he states, *"Not that I speak in regard to need, for I have learned in whatever state I am, to be content: I know how to be abased, and I know how to abound. Everywhere and in all things I have learned both to be full and to be hungry, both to abound and to suffer need. I can do all things through Christ who strengthens me."*

The writer of Hebrews puts the challenge in these words: *"Let your conduct be without covetousness; be content with such things as you have. For He Himself has said, "I will never leave you nor forsake you"* (Hebrews 13:5).

God will give us strength to control money and materialism and to empower us to live lives of godliness and contentment. If we don't allow Him to strengthen us in this area, then we will face unnecessary temptation and possible consequences. Paul said, *"But those who desire to be rich fall* *into temptation and a snare, and into many foolish and harmful lusts which drown men in destruction and perdition. <u>For the love of money is a root of all kinds of evil, for which some have strayed from the faith in their greediness, and pierced themselves through with many sorrows</u>"* (1 Timothy 6:9-10).

Please note that the love of money can lead us to ruin, destruction, departure from the Christian faith, and inflict us with much heartache.

There is nothing inherently wrong with money. It can be a great tool. It is how we view and use it that determines if we please God or not. When the Lord financially prospers His children, it is not for the purpose of continually spending it on ourselves and our families, but to be generous to others in need of the Gospel and the basics of life.

GIVING FROM A GENEROUS HEART

If we're honest, we must all confess that we have made mistakes dealing with money. As a result, many of us have misused His resources, are in debt, and have a difficult time serving God unencumbered. Please don't feel condemned, but we all need to be convicted in this area. Our objective should be to eliminate excessive debt and place ourselves in a position of being generous givers and not borrowers.

The prophet Malachi called out the priests of Israel for robbing God because they stopped giving to the Lord. The people of Israel found themselves in trouble when they followed the leadership's lifestyle of withholding from God what was rightfully His.

Even though we do not live under the Old Covenant, the principle still remains because God does not change. Many of us in the Church are robbing God because we are taking most (if not everything) He has given to us and spending it on ourselves instead of considering it all His to accomplish the mission He has ordained for us. There are tremendous physical and spiritual needs in the world. God has given the Church all that is necessary to address these needs if we will be obedient in our giving.

It is essential that we deal with this aspect of finances straight up, head-on, instead of evading the subject or offering an excuse for our behavior. We must not allow money or materialism to master us—these things must be under the control of the Holy Spirit. We can make the decision to give our first-fruits to Him regularly because we *desire* to, we are *privileged* and *delighted* to—not because we *have* to. Our choice should reflect a generous, open heart.

Of course, we must take care of ourselves and provide for our families, but also finance the Kingdom of God so the Church might continue to achieve the Great Commission and please our Heavenly Father.

A GOAL TO LIVE AS A GIVER

God used tithing under the Old Covenant as a requirement in order for the citizens of Israel to function physically and spiritually as a nation. The Christian Church is referred to as a holy nation (1 Peter 2:9) which also has a clear function to fulfill. Under the New Covenant, we certainly don't promote the tithe as a requirement, but as a model for the church to use to fulfill Her mission of evangelism, discipleship, and ministry to the poor and those in need.

The emphasis of this book is not to debate tithing in the New Testament church. Even though the New Covenant does not emphasize a specific amount, we do have tithing as an example for us in the Old Covenant. Jesus' teachings always raised the requirements of the Law...to the heart level.

Under grace, may we all <u>desire</u> to give at least a tithe and aspire to give more—not because we *have* to, but because we want to *from our hearts*. Can you imagine how the world would be impacted for Christ if all His children gave like this? When we do, the mission of Christ becomes ours!

Jesus instructed the Pharisees to tithe, but not to neglect justice, mercy, and faith (Matthew 23:23). Our giving reflects our hearts.

Giving is a heart issue, not just a money issue. God used one of the tithes under the old covenant to teach the Israelites to learn to *"fear the Lord always"* (Deuteronomy 14:22-23). Again, though not a requirement today, the principle of tithing from our increase teaches us to fear (revere and honor) our Lord with what He has given to us and keeps our priorities in check with His.

Proverbs 3:9-10 instructs us to honor the Lord with all our possessions and the first fruits of our increased blessings. The context was for the agricultural nation of Israel who literally gave from their crops to the storehouse in the temple. This principle still applies to us today in giving the "first fruits" of our increased blessings (our paychecks) to our Lord through His Church.

When someone really wants to know if we are committed to a cause, we may hear the phrase, "Put your money where your mouth is." Are there any causes greater than Kingdom causes? In today's system, a tithe of your first fruits would simply be a tenth of your income. We can say we love Him with our mouths, but when we systematically give Him back His money, it proves that we love and fear Him. Our giving is also a way to show God who truly serves Him and who does not (Malachi 3:16-18). Giving from a thankful heart is an act of worship.

There is a distinction between those who <u>say</u> they love God and the ones who <u>show</u> they do. When we financially give, it honors our Lord, it enables the Church to fulfill Her mission and it blesses us both here and in heaven.

Living under grace should motivate us to give bountifully with a cheerful heart to accomplish the mission God has given us (2 Corinthians 9:6-11). Grace keeps us from becoming legalistic and it causes us to give beyond any specific percentage of giving. We give, not because of a religious duty or a "have-to" mentality, but because we desire to. Never forget, *"It is more blessed to give than to receive"* (Acts 20:35).

SOWING AND REAPING

Contentment and giving are the greatest antidotes for greed and materialism. May a spirit of contentment and generosity flood your heart.

In 2 Corinthians 9:10-11 we read, *"Now he who supplies seed to the sower and bread for food will also supply and increase your store of seed and will enlarge the harvest of your righteousness.* <u>*You will be made rich in every way so that you can be generous on every occasion, and through us your generosity will result in thanksgiving to God"*</u> (NIV).

As we sow (give back) the seed that He supplies, He desires to enrich us in order for us to be even more generous in every way. I refer to this as biblical prosperity—prospering to be a blessing.

Working hard and making money is biblical and we should be thankful for the opportunity. God blesses His children to be a blessing! We have to have money before we can give money. Remember, money is not bad. It is the love of money that leads us to destruction. Let us purpose in our hearts to use money for eternal purposes. Let us position ourselves to become generous givers to Kingdom causes.

According to the Scriptures, when we sow bountifully, we will reap bountifully. As we give more to God, we reap more...to give more, etc. We will reap what we sow on earth...and in heaven. This is why we must always sow (give) with a cheerful and thankful heart. God loves a cheerful giver (2 Corinthians 9:6-7)!

In a culture of materialism, the Lord calls us to be different—to be good stewards, to manage well the resources with which He has entrusted us. God is not a kill-joy. He is not against us enjoying the material items He blesses us with. Our heavenly Father simply does not want those items to control us. He has not called us to guilt...but to be a blessing (1 Timothy 6:17-19).

The Lord gave me a personal experience around this issue. It began with His gift to me...a heart for the poor. I have lived with great passion for God's heart in this area and at one time would unfairly judge people who did not have the same level of conviction. I felt guilty for the blessings of God—knowing the suffering of people in my own city, country and the world. I really struggled with having material blessings.

I have had opportunities to spend time in third world countries. One of those opportunities was a trip to Sudan, Africa. I saw extreme poverty first-hand, the need for basic food and clothing. Literally, people (some with clothing, some without) would come out of the bush in search of life-sustaining resources —a blanket for cover—a morsel of food. How God's heart must break! We must respond!

After the ministry there was completed, my co-workers and I gathered in a restaurant in the nearest city and sat down for dinner. I ordered a nice meal. As the plate was set down before me, the guilt was overwhelming! I could not imagine putting a bite of that food in my mouth. I was unable to eat.

The guilt held me burdened and sorrowful. Then the Lord spoke very clearly to my heart, "I have not called you to guilt. I have blessed you to be a blessing! Now rise up and eat"— and man, did I eat!

The burden and passion for God's heart for the poor remains strong and growing to this very day, but the guilt for being blessed is gone. Now I desire His blessing so I can be a blessing to my immediate family, my church family, and the world. Thank You, Lord!

Enjoy a simple life (don't judge others in their definition of this). Be thankful for what He has given to you and give all you can to the Kingdom of God—where your investment will never return void. Using God's money His way will bring Him and you tremendous pleasure!

To Sum it Up

In our homes, our marriages need to function the way God has ordained. If we are single, we must use our homes and relationships to glorify Him and advance His Kingdom.

We learned that men need to live as God has called them (as His sons, as godly husbands and fathers), continually growing in their relationship with the Lord; to lead and love their wives; to father their children well; to have their finances under control (realizing that they are stewards of God's money).

Women, too, must live as God has called them (as His daughters, as godly wives and mothers), also developing their relationship with the Lord, giving help and respect to their husbands. They are also to mother their children well; to partner with their husbands in having their finances under control so they can be good and faithful stewards of God's resources.

Can you imagine how living by God's Word in our homes will position us to disciple someone else in the faith? This frees us to love and serve the Church and the world. We will not be able to fulfill the final two foundations if we don't have the first two in proper order. It would be hypocritical.

If we attempt to love and serve the church before loving

and ministering to Christ and our families, <u>we have it all
backwards</u>. However, if we have these in order (not
flawlessly, but faithfully) we position ourselves to not only
love and serve the church, but also the world.

ARE YOU PREPARED TO LEAD?

No man or woman should be considered for any
leadership function in the church until they have become
faithful in the first two foundations (Living in Love and Service
to <u>Christ</u>, and in the <u>Home</u>).

If we are not spending time alone with our Lord, what can
we possibly offer to others spiritually? If our homes,
singleness, marriages, children, and finances are not in order,
how can we teach and model for others how a Christian
home should function.

Some churches have a poor reputation due to leaders
who don't have these first two foundations in order (or
practice them) —yet they are trying to lead others.

Remember, Jesus challenged the religious people of His
day who had plenty of head knowledge, but their lives did
not reflect godly principles.

Today, two thousand years later, it is still necessary for us
to evaluate our lives in the light of our Lord's Word. We need
to ask God to convict our hearts; allowing the Holy Spirit to
empower us to repent, ask for forgiveness if necessary, and
make changes. May this process cause our homes to be filled
with His presence and peace.

REFLECT AND RESPOND

Single:
- How are you using your God-given gifts and skills to further the Kingdom?

- Evaluate how you are honoring God in your home and relationships.

- In what area(s) do you need to grow and mature?

Married:
- How are you fulfilling your God-given role and responsibility as a husband/wife?

- Evaluate your spiritual, emotional, and physical intimacy with each other.

- What changes are needed?

Parents:
- Evaluate your parenting and the relationship that you currently have with your children (and your grandchildren). What changes would you make?

- Do you constantly pray for, love, and attempt to connect with your children?

- Are you walking with your children, modeling the Living on Target lifestyle and passing it on to them?

Finances:
- As His steward, are you ready to give an account to God of how you view and use His money?

- Where is your treasure?

- Have you personally owned Christ's mission? How is this reflected in your giving?

- If you are in excessive debt, what is your specific plan to eliminate the financial pressure?

- Since all you have is the Lord's, what is your view of tithing (10%) and giving offerings to Him to further His Kingdom? If you aren't doing that, when will you begin?

Unless we ask the Lord to build our home, we are laboring in vain.

FIVE

FOUNDATION #3

LIVING IN LOVE AND SERVICE TO THE CHURCH

Now, therefore, you are no longer strangers and foreigners, but fellow citizens with the saints and members of the household of God.

— EPHESIANS 2:19

The word *church* is the Greek word *ekklesia*. It means "a called out assembly"—those who have exchanged the darkness of their sin for His marvelous light.

To this very day, the Church is the greatest organism on the planet. It is not a building or a place, rather the Church is the people of God.

Certainly we have our challenges, yet the Lord views us as His prized possession. He loves the Church with an extreme love…so much so that He died for Her. He has also called us to cherish and serve the Church with all of our hearts.

It is vital that we develop a true love not only for the Universal Church, but also our local Church and particularly for that part of it to which we belong.

We need to love the Body of Christ of which we are a part. Shouldn't every pastor and member of a local congregation believe that their church is awesome and life-giving? I certainly do!

This doesn't mean that you look past situations which need to be addressed. There will be challenges in every congregation, because there are humans involved. But it is essential that we love the Church and that we stop chronically complaining against Her.

It is necessary to pray for the leadership and not gossip about them. Share with them and other mature believers the issues or concerns that are troubling you, but determine to become part of the solution instead of being a part of the problem. Because of our love for Christ and each other we need to address any issues that would hinder our unity.

There may be times you have prayerfully dealt with all the issues you could and you still must leave a local congregation. Please don't depart with bitterness. Remember that we, who have placed our faith in Christ alone, are all brothers and sisters, even with our differences and challenges.

THE BRIDE OF CHRIST

Never forget that Jesus died for the Church, whom He calls, His Bride. If we love the *Bridegroom*, we really need to love His wife—the *Bride* (which is all of us as believers). As mature disciples, we will overflow with love for the universal Church and for the local Church. We will want to serve His Bride with our time, spiritual gifts, talents, and finances.

As we disciple people in the faith, it is important that we mentor them in truly loving the Church. There will be plenty of challenges with the potential of conflict, doctrinal disagreement, leadership issues, integrity questions, hypocrisy, and problems of sin. Even so, we have a baseline: the fact that the Body of Christ (the Church), is the Bride of Christ…and we must learn how to love Her!

There are some who attempt to serve the Church, but have lost their love for Her. May we see and care for the Church the way Christ does—to press through the issues that hinder us and purpose to love the Bride of Christ (see "Peace and Reconciliation Begins with You" in chapter 3).

Those who have been hurt by the Church must learn to embrace Her again and be loved by Her in return. Those who may have harmed the Church must seek forgiveness and reconciliation. For some, both apply. Our witness to the world is on the line.

Could you consider yourself one of the Church's biggest fans? Many of us are sports fans and we cheer for our favorite team. I believe it would truly please our Lord if we became fans of the Church and cheered Her on as the greatest team on earth.

THE UNIFIED CHURCH

Jesus stated that the world would know we are His disciples by our love for one another (John 13:34-35). As vital as evangelism, preaching, and doctrine are, Jesus said that we would be identified first and foremost as His disciples because of our love for one another. Jesus has given the world a standard to use to evaluate if we are truly His...our love for each another...Wow! How are we doing? How are *you* doing in this area?

As we put this love into practice, it gives a clear witness that we truly have been saved by Jesus Christ. Our Lord prayed to His Father in John 17:20-23 that we in the Church would live as one; Jew, Gentile, black, white, Latino, African, Asian, etc., all as one.

Jesus desired that all of His followers would live and worship in unity and not allow anything to divide us. All the races have been called to live together as one unified body, to break down any walls of denominationalism, racism, sexism, classism—all of those "isms" should fall at the foot of the cross.

"I do not pray for these alone, but also for those who will believe in Me through their word; that they all may be one, as You, Father, are in Me, and I in You; that they also may be one in Us, <u>that the world may believe that You sent Me.</u> And the glory which You gave Me I have given them, that they may be one just as We are one: I in them, and You in Me; that they may be made perfect in one, <u>and that the world may know that You have sent Me</u>, and have loved them as You have loved Me" (John 17:20-23).

Christ desired that we as His sons and daughters in the Church would live unified lives in true love for one another. This is extremely important to God, for our witness, and for our experience on Judgment Day (see "Abounding Love" in Chapter 2).

According to Scripture, the foremost evangelistic tool we have is our unity in Christ. God's Word records how Jesus prayed, not once but twice that His future believers would be one in Him, <u>so that</u> the world would believe the Father had sent Him. Until this is completed, may we make every effort to keep the unity of the Spirit through the bond of peace (Ephesians 4:3). There is <u>one</u> body in Christ!

Unity does not come at the cost of heresy or unrepentant habitual sinful behavior—but all other issues should be pressed through for our unity to remain strong. <u>His reputation is measured by our unity</u>!

We must disciple people in this crucial area. We are called to *be* the Church, not just *attend* church.

Multi-ethnic, Multi-cultural Church Movement

"And they sang a new song, saying: 'You are worthy to take the scroll, and to open its seals; For You were slain, and <u>have redeemed us to God by Your blood out of every tribe and tongue and people and nation</u>, and have made us kings and priests to our God; And we shall reign on the earth" (Revelation 5:9-10).

By these verses we see clearly that all people from all around the world will be represented in heaven. His Church on earth must reflect the same inclusion while we wait for this prophecy to be literally fulfilled.

The following verses from Ephesians 2:14-16 have already come to pass: *"For He Himself is our peace, who has made* *both one, and has broken down the middle wall of separation, having abolished in His flesh the enmity, that is, the law of commandments contained in ordinances, so as <u>to create in Himself one new man from the two</u>, thus making peace, and that He might reconcile them both to God in <u>one body</u> through the cross, thereby putting to death the enmity"* (Ephesians 2:14-16).

In the early church, there was enmity—a "wall" or division between the Jewish and the Gentile communities. In Christ, by breaking down all walls, He has now created one new people, His one Church...that we might live peaceful lives together, thus creating our witness to the world.

The interpretation here is between Jew and Gentile. Our application of these verses can certainly include the "wall" between all races.

Isn't it time to put an end to division and hostility? We worship the same Lord, yet our prejudices and preferences have kept us segregated within the confines of the Church. "Equal, but separate" has been quoted by some in the Body of Christ, but this quote is not found in the Bible. Surely this must break our Lord's heart!

After some Gentiles were saved in the house of Cornelius (Acts 10), the Jewish believers began to debate how to connect them into the Church. For some people, those discussions of how to unite various races into the local congregation continue to this very day. Others fail to wrestle with it at all. It is very clear from Scripture that it should be a priority for all Christians to consider how to live out their faith <u>together</u> as the unified Body of Christ.

We know from Scripture that the walls of division

between Jew and Gentile and all races and cultures have been removed in Christ for over 2000 years. What has kept us from experiencing what Christ has already accomplished, and is still desiring for His church? Certainly continued prejudices, preferences, and non-submissive attitudes are high on the list.

These characteristics must be crucified for the reality of unity to advance and mature. There are indeed, an increasing number of Christians and Church leaders today who desire to see our Lord's Church look on earth as we know it will be in heaven...where every tribe, language, people, and nation is represented (Revelation 5:9-10).

There are more and more churches who (remaining true to Scripture) are attempting to remove labels and barriers, creating an atmosphere of total inclusion. For the first time in the history of the Church, we are seeing this bearing fruit in greater measure than ever before. Praise the Lord!

How Now Shall We Live Together?

Paul said, " *"Therefore if there is any consolation in Christ, if any comfort of love, if any fellowship of the Spirit, if any affection and mercy, fulfill my joy by being like-minded, having the same love, being of one accord, of one mind. Let nothing be done through selfish ambition or conceit, but in lowliness of mind let each esteem others better than himself. Let each of you look out not only for his own interests, but also for the interests of others"* (Philippians 2:1-4).

Please notice that we must humble ourselves and consider others not just equal but "better" than ourselves. This attitude can only be achieved by the power of the Holy Spirit.

151

There is a huge difference between tolerating others and truly accepting them. People know when they're being tolerated and when they are being accepted. Paul exhorts us not only to accept people, but to esteem others better than ourselves.

When Christians stop judging their fellow man according to the flesh and truly begin to view others as better than themselves, then our Lord's desire for His Church will be accomplished. This can—and is happening today!

I have observed this movement in the congregation where I have served for over twelve years. It has been the most wonderful and challenging journey of my life. I _love_ the Church and I believe She is a beautiful expression of the Kingdom of Heaven on earth. This environment doesn't just happen. We are continually loving, learning, and mutually submitting one to another as a family of believers. It's beautiful!

We are a racially diverse congregation with approximately fifty nations represented. In order to be part of our local church, _everyone_ has to give up some preferences. We have learned and are still learning how to temper our personal choices (in music, worship style, church structure, language, dress, etc.) to esteem others better than than ourselves. We will continue to mature in this process.

Loving and serving our fellow man has always been part of the call of the Gospel and it should be a high value for the Church. When this is authentically lived out, it creates an atmosphere where _everyone_ feels welcome and at home. This has always been our Lord's desire for His Church. Jesus Himself taught His disciples saying, _"Is it not written, 'My house shall be called a house of prayer for all nations' [races]?"_ (Mark 11:17).

Our local congregations should reflect the Kingdom of God. We know that it is not natural for different races and cultures to live life together and to worship together in the same church, but we don't walk in the natural. We walk by the supernatural and it truly causes the world to ponder how this could be. We hope they will observe the love in the Church for one another and that they'll have to declare to themselves that truly the Father has sent the Son (John 17). AMEN!

Lord, give us spiritual eyes to see people as You see them. Help us to love, respond to, and embrace them with Your heart, for the sake of Your reputation and to reach those who are lost. All for Your glory!

One final note on this subject: Please do not put yourself or your church under pressure to force a multi-ethic/cultural congregation into being. It certainly is a biblical goal, but God must achieve this. I submit to you to practice the Kingdom principles noted above so as not to hinder anyone from experiencing God's love and acceptance in your congregation. We cannot make the races and cultures come together, but we can hinder this from happening. We are responsible for our actions and attitudes as we trust God to add to His church as He wills.

Love the way He loves and leave the growth and diversity to Him. Our Lord will be pleased with churches that love like this regardless of racial make-up. Remember, the Church belongs to Him.

FIVE AREAS OF FOCUS

The following five areas are significant to the Body of Christ. Let us examine each one in light of our own involvement and commitment:

1. COMMUNITY

As the Body of Christ, we are to live life together. In Acts 2:42-47 the early Church:

- Learned together
- Praised God and prayed together
- Shared meals and communion in their homes together
- Lived relationally in community together

Our goal is not to duplicate the cultural context of the early church but instead to strive for the same objectives in our culture today.

It seems that the first area of our life which suffers because of our fast-paced schedule is in the area of relationships: with God, our families, believers within the Church, and people in the world. Every person in a Christian fellowship needs relationships that will encourage and equip them in their faith. It is an essential ingredient for our spiritual maturity and development.

The Bible cautions, *"Beware brethren lest there be in any of you an evil heart of unbelief in departing from the living God; but exhort one another daily while it is called today, least any of you be hardened through the deceitfulness of sin. For we have become partakers of Christ if we hold the beginning of our confidence steadfast to the end"* (Hebrews 3:12-14).

The word "exhort" means we are to come along side of

and encourage one another. We should regularly speak into each others' lives with godly counsel, appreciation, love, and prayer. Each of us could use more of this support.

Please note from this verse that sin is deceitful. We all have blind spots and we need our brothers and sisters in Christ to help us with our weaknesses. We need others to encourage us to arrest sin and live out our righteousness. Without that, our hearts can drift and eventually become so hardened that we may be tempted to depart from the living God. If our spiritual lives begin to decline, it is extremely important that we are living in such closeness with fellow believers that they notice and can bring it to our attention. Can you honestly say that you have these kinds of relationships within the church? They are vital!

THE IMPACT OF SMALL GROUPS

The enemy loves to pick-off, accuse, and destroy isolated believers. We were not meant to live the Christian life alone.

When a country is at war, their army lives, eats, trains, and fights together against their common enemy. They battle side by side because it is a matter of victory or defeat, of physical life or death.

It is no different with our spiritual lives. We are involved in spiritual warfare (2 Corinthians 10:3-5) with a very real enemy and his demons of darkness. We should never drift away from our band of brothers and sisters in Christ. Our enemy is like a sniper who loves to pick off isolated believers who drift away (emotionally, spiritually, or physically) from God and from the army of God. Stay alert! It is a matter of spiritual victory or defeat and a matter of spiritual life and death. We are called to fight the good fight of faith <u>together</u>!

Please realize that you can't be intimately acquainted with a large number of people even if you worship in the same location each week. The Bible exhorts us to live out the "one anothers." Submit to one another, pray for one another, encourage one another, serve one another, exhort one another, etc. This is why we support small groups within churches...so that we can live out the *"one anothers"* of Scripture.

As we make it our aim to be well pleasing to God, we believe that every Christian should make a commitment to be a part of a small community of believers. These are safe havens where people can be honest and open—to receive prayer and be cared for as they journey through this life.

We need to pray for one another on a regular basis. Our enemy seeks to kill, steal, and destroy us. Life itself comes at us fast...with all its unpredictable challenges and struggles. There is not a person on this planet who doesn't need prayer!

Pride, laziness, or gossip will keep people from praying for one another, which is exactly what our enemy desires. Our adversary doesn't want anyone to be healed...but our God does! *"<u>Therefore confess your sins to each other and pray for each other so that you may be healed.</u> The prayer of a righteous man is powerful and effective"* (James 5:16 NIV).

God desires to see His children healed physically, emotionally and spiritually. If the Church would create safe places for individuals to confess sin and various struggles...and to sincerely pray for one another, we should expect more lives to be healed. This is the environment that God desires for His Church.

Do you gather with a safe small group on a regular basis? Are you helpful in creating those environments? In your congregation, who are you praying for regularly and who is praying for you? A small group should be a haven where your brothers and sisters can help carry burdens to our Lord and where everyone can be equipped to Live on Target together. If you're not involved in a small group, join one (or start one) for your benefit and for the benefit of others.

REAL CHRISTIANS

Allow me to share just one example of what takes place as a result of small groups:

> *A couple joined our church and became involved in a Home Fellowship where the Living on Target discipleship was taught and modeled. As the Scriptures were read about a particular topic, people shared from their hearts about where they stood personally in relationship to that topic.*
>
> *As men expressed their struggles concerning being the spiritual leader in their homes and how they found it difficult to pray with their wives, the other men would encourage them and gather around to lay hands on them and pray that the Holy Spirit would empower them to lead their homes in a Godly manner. Men would follow up between the meetings to check on the progress and provide additional encouragement and sometimes just listen.*
>
> *This couple got to see real life, real Christians*

overcoming real problems with a real Holy Spirit!

WE NEED EACH OTHER

These safe places—where people can gather to be taught and equipped in the Scriptures, encouraged, loved, and even corrected—become vital, not only for those who are already in the Church, but for individuals who are being convicted to come to Christ and become part of a fellowship of believers.

Many are drawn out of sinful lifestyles having lived under tremendous emotional and sometimes even physical bondage. It is of utmost importance that we in the church create places for people to come and be healed without being judged or feeling that they will be condemned. When men and women come to the church broken and repentant, may we accept them as Christ does. The church must love and minister the way Jesus did!

I believe if we were to live in community together for a span of thirty years, we would not only celebrate life's joys (births, weddings, etc.), but also comfort each other in the challenges and disappointments of our journey. We need each other in both good and difficult times.

I have observed some "mature" believers who opt out of the community life of the church. There are those who don't believe that they need other people—they only need God. And many simply don't take time to invest in other members of the congregation. We know that the Lord is to be our source of life, but He has instructed us to live life together and disciple others.

Mature believers need to make themselves available to live life with and disciple the younger and less mature in the Faith. <u>Everyone</u> needs to be prayed for, cared for, and equipped in the Scriptures. Therefore, <u>everyone</u> is needed!

As we grow, we may excel in one area and lag behind in another. As a result we become unbalanced. It is wonderful to have other like-minded brothers and sisters who can gently call this to our attention. This is one of the many benefits of a small group. By being involved in such a group we provide ourselves with encouragement to stay on target.

We are in a spiritual battle for the souls and maturity of men and women so that all will end their race of faith strong. I am asking you to pray for and cheer each other on to the finish line…<u>together</u>!

2. COMMUNION

As we aim to be well pleasing in living life in community with one another, we need to look at the early Church as our example. One aspect of the Christian walk that was actually practiced in small groups in their homes was communion (or the Lord's Supper).

1 Corinthians 11:17-34 is the only reference in the New Testament giving instructions about the Lord's Supper—and it was corrective in nature. The church at Corinth was not honoring the Lord or His Supper properly. May we learn from their mistakes. First, we see that communion was a command of our Lord: *"Do this in remembrance of me"* (verse 24).

For approximately the first three hundred years of Church history, believers took communion in the home. We also practice communion in our Home Fellowship groups. It provides an intimate environment, one in which fellow believers can unite and enjoy a meal together. The Bible refers to this as a love feast. In the South we call them "pot-luck suppers" where everybody brings food, and benefits from fellowship.

There is enjoyment of relationships, laughter, and encouragement. Then before, during, or after the meal, we pause, examine our hearts, pray, and worship, focusing on what the Lord's Supper represents as we share the bread and cup together. This is how we proclaim, as the Scriptures teach, "the Lord's death until He comes."

It is essential that every Christian participate in the Lord's Supper on a regular basis. The Bible does not mandate a specific time or frequency; our only directive is to do this in remembrance of Him.

Acknowledging and proclaiming His death brings our attention and focus on what our Lord accomplished for us on the cross. We certainly celebrate His resurrection and His life within us, yet we are clearly instructed to remember His death through participating in this memorial. This honors and pleases Him.

There were dire consequences for not taking communion seriously and many were bringing judgment on themselves. The apostle Paul described that many were becoming sick, feeble, and some even died by not discerning the Lord's body properly (1 Corinthians 11:30). These dire consequences can be avoided by examining ourselves with an honest self-examination and confession of sin. Paul told us to judge ourselves so that the Lord would not have to (1 Corinthians 11:31-32).

Wow! God is very serious about this memorial and how we approach it. The consequences of not discerning the Lord's body properly are enormous. Is it possible that some of our anemic witness and lack of passion for the Lord is a direct result of our disobedience to the command to observe the Lord's Supper properly?

His instructions are clear. We must heed and obey them. There should be no excuse for any true believer not to take communion with a pure and thankful heart on a regular basis. This is an essential part of our Christianity. May the Holy Spirit convict us all to participate with passion, conviction, and holy fear.

3. CORPORATE WORSHIP

Joshua, one of the leaders of the nation of Israel, gathered all the tribes of Israel together. He exhorted them to put away the foreign gods of their fathers and choose whom they would serve. Joshua then made his famous statement, which needs to be echoed by every believer today: *"As for me and my house, we will serve the Lord"* (Joshua 24:15).

Every household should make it their practice to serve our Lord daily and to worship Him together as a family on a weekly basis.

We are being tempted with all types of entertainment, sporting events, shopping—the list of attractions is long indeed. Yet, the Scriptures say, *"Let us hold fast the confession of our hope without wavering, for He who* *promised is faithful. And let us consider one another in order to stir up love and good works, <u>not forsaking the assembling of ourselves together, as is the manner of some, but exhorting one another, and so much the more as you see the Day approaching</u>"* (Hebrews 10:23-25).

As we gather together, we can pray, read the Word, and worship—lifting our hearts, voices, and hands as one. This is a picture of Jesus' desire for us to be one as He and the Father are One. This not only glorifies the God we love and serve, it also blesses the saints and draws the unsaved to Him. Meeting together is to be both corporate (the entire congregation) and in small groups.

We are to unite together as a family of believers weekly, making it a part of our lifestyle. Our children should not be asking, "if" we are going to church this weekend. It should already be ingrained in them that "As for me and my house, we will not only serve the Lord, but we will worship Him as a family every week, joining together with our local congregation of believers." Is this your practice and habit?

FIVE ASPECTS OF CORPORATE WORSHIP

God has established the corporate gathering of believers with purposeful intention. Please evaluate your participation in the following aspects of corporate worship:

Giving a greeting of love:

There is something powerful about the expression of mutual affection exchanged among believers. It emphasizes the motivation under which we operate—love. First, the love we experience from God, then the love that overflows to our brothers and sisters in Christ (1 Corinthians 16:20).

Giving our worship to God:

Though we express our worship personally in countless ways during the week, lifting our voices *corporately* to Him reflects our desire to live in agreement with Jesus' prayer that we be one—as He and the Father are One. We honor Him when we worship the Lord together in the beauty of holiness (Psalm 29:2).

Giving our tithes and offerings as an act of our worship:

This is a time set aside to worship God through our giving. It is our joy to present our finances for Kingdom purposes (Proverbs 3:9-10). Meeting together regularly establishes a method for obeying and sharing in the delight of giving (1 Corinthians 16:2).

Receiving His Word:

Sitting together under the teaching and preaching of God's Word gives us understanding and biblical guidance. His Word is living and powerful and, when applied, will equip us for the work God has called us to do. When we know the truth, it will set us and keep us—free!

We give ourselves the opportunity, letting the Holy Spirit work in our hearts, to be convicted, encouraged, burdened, blessed, challenged, and affirmed. We build familiarity with, knowledge of, and insight into His precious Word to us (2 Timothy 3:16).

Giving ourselves to serve others:

Corporate gatherings should include the opportunity to

serve each other. Our service may include teaching, prayer ministry, the ministry of helps, the children's ministry, etc. We should be available as willing servants to serve the Church and the world.

We must also remember to receive what is offered from fellow believers. None of us are excluded from needing the gifts of the Body of Christ. The reciprocal blessings of the act of serving help keep us humble, integrated, and appreciative of each other and of the God who designed us to live in community (Hebrews 10:24-25).

Notice that four of the five aspects of corporate worship involve giving. In cultural Christianity, people seem to come to Church meetings only to receive. Even as we give in the four aspects of worship, we certainly receive a blessing from our Lord. When we receive His Word, we are constantly empowered and strengthened to continually love, serve and give more. Is this your perspective in corporate worship?

4. MINISTRY TO THE POOR

God's heart and concern for those in physical need is clear in both covenants (Old and New Testaments). More than four hundred verses speak about God's passion for those in need. His desire is that His followers would share His deep concern.

Jesus was so burdened over how the poor were treated that Matthew tells us we will be judged by how we minister to them. Jesus declares:

When the Son of Man comes in His glory, and all the holy angels with Him, then He will sit on the throne of His glory. All the nations will be gathered before Him, and He will separate them one from another, as a shepherd divides his sheep from the goats. And He will set the sheep on His right hand, but the goats on the left.

Then the King will say to those on His right hand, "Come, you blessed of My Father, inherit the kingdom prepared for you from the foundation of the world: for I was hungry and you gave Me food; I was thirsty and you gave Me drink; I was a stranger and you took Me in; I was naked and you clothed Me; I was sick and you visited Me; I was in prison and you came to Me."

Then the righteous will answer Him, saying, "Lord, when did we see You hungry and feed You, or thirsty and give You drink? When did we see You a stranger and take You in, or naked and clothe You? Or when did we see You sick, or in prison, and come to You?"

And the King will answer and say to them, "Assuredly, I say to you, inasmuch as you did it to one of the least of these My brethren, you did it to Me."

Then He will also say to those on the left hand, "Depart from Me, you cursed, into the everlasting fire prepared for the devil and his angels: for I was hungry and you gave Me no food; I was thirsty and you gave Me no drink; I was a stranger and you did not take Me in, naked and you did not clothe Me, sick and in prison and you did not visit Me."

Then they also will answer Him, saying, "Lord, when did we see You hungry or thirsty or a stranger or naked or sick or in prison, and did not minister to You?"

Then He will answer them, saying, <u>"Assuredly, I say to you, inasmuch as you did not do it to one of the least of these, you did not do it to Me." And these will go away into everlasting punishment, but the righteous into eternal life"</u> (Matthew 25:31-46).

That's powerful! It seems very clear in this passage that serving those in need proves our faith in Christ. James 1:22 says to *"<u>be doers of the word, and not hearers only, deceiving yourselves.</u>"* And a few verses later, James is exhorting us to meet the needs of the orphans and widows. He continues, *"<u>Pure and undefiled religion</u> before God and the Father is this: <u>to visit orphans and widows in their trouble</u>, and to keep oneself unspotted from the world"* (James 1:27). Throughout Scripture we are commanded to take care of those in need.

"IN DEED AND IN TRUTH"

Our heart is assured of our love relationship with God when it overflows in deliberate acts of love and truth. The Father's abiding love in the believer *will*, of necessity, show itself by caring action.

Here is how this is expressed by John: *"By this we know love, because He laid down His life for us. And we also ought to lay down our lives for the brethren. But whoever has this world's goods, and sees his brother in need, and shuts up his heart from him, how does the love of God abide in him? My little children, let us not love in word or in tongue, but in deed and in truth. And by this we know that we are of the truth, and shall assure our hearts before Him"* (1 John 3:16-19).

Long ago, King Solomon wrote: *"He who oppresses the poor reproaches his Maker, but he who honors Him has mercy on the needy"* (Proverbs 14: 31). Can it be any clearer?

God's heart is extremely merciful and compassionate toward the poor, and if we are disciples Living on Target, we will share His deep concern. Our actions will reflect our joint passion (with God) for the needy.

Although our ministry to the poor includes loving and serving the lost who are in need, it starts with caring for our own brothers and sisters (the Church). As Paul writes, *"Therefore, as we have opportunity, let us do good to all, especially to those who are of the household of faith"* (Galatians 6:10).

As we live for the glory of God, our desire as Christians should be to assist anyone in need for the glory of God, not bypassing that we are instructed to help those in the Church first.

Father, may we give and use Your resources in a manner that will do good to all and will bring glory to Your Name. Give us a heart for the poor and those in need.

5. THE PERSECUTED CHURCH

In Living in Love and Service to the Church, I believe we must also include the necessity to grow in our love for the persecuted church.

In America, we have tremendous freedom when it comes to our faith. This is not the case in many countries in our world. The Bible gives this admonition: *"Remember the prisoners as if chained with them—those who are mistreated—since you yourselves are in the body also"* (Hebrews 13:3).

There are many in our family of believers around the globe who are suffering simply because they are Christians. Much of the Church in foreign nations is forced to gather underground. They cannot freely, publicly express their love and adoration to Christ as their Lord and Savior.

Sadly, believers are being persecuted, arrested, beaten, sentenced to prison, and many are being martyred because of their faith in our Lord Jesus Christ.

In America, we sometimes talk about "suffering for Christ," but we must make a clear distinction between our mere inconveniences compared to the true suffering that is experienced by so many of our brothers and sisters living in the four corners of the earth. However, even in America, the more we stand for Christ, the more we will experience persecution at some level.

We must prepare for this persecution to increase as we approach the return of Christ. Remember the words of the

Apostle Paul, *"Yes...all who desire to live godly in Christ Jesus will suffer persecution"* (2 Timothy 3:12).

Scripture also records, *"...when they had called for the apostles and beaten them, they commanded that they should not speak in the name of Jesus, and let them go. So they departed from the presence of the council, rejoicing that they were counted worthy to suffer shame for His name. And daily in the temple, and in every house, they did not cease teaching and preaching Jesus as the Christ"* (Acts 7:40-42).

Following our Lord will cost us (Luke 14:25-33), but He is absolutely worth it. He suffered for us...may we stand for Him at all cost!

PRAY FOR THOSE WHO SUFFER

We are called as The Church (the Body of Christ) to live our lives as true disciples of Christ! The Bible tells us in 1 Corinthians 12 that if one of our members suffers, we all should suffer with him or her. If one of our members rejoices, we are also to rejoice.

This is the picture, not only of the local congregation, but also of the Universal Church. In order for us to mature as believers, we must see the Body of Christ the way our Lord does. It is bigger than any physical location and She continues to expand around the world. Yet in many nations, She is greatly suffering.

Please pray for, support, and stand with our brothers and sisters who are being persecuted even today. They are our family, and families rejoice and suffer together...come quickly Lord Jesus!

TO SUM IT UP

There are countless ways to love and effectively serve the Church. Living out these five areas as a lifestyle with the unified Body of Christ will bring great pleasure to our Lord.

Make a commitment to assemble regularly with those God has joined you with, to corporately worship as a family and take communion on a regular basis with fellow believers the way Jesus has commanded us to. This lifestyle will set an example and leave a legacy for our children and grandchildren.

Let me encourage you to live in community with other Christians by joining a small group where you are known by name and can fellowship with and pray for others personally.

We need to accept our privilege and responsibility in creating a safe place where any person can come and feel welcomed and loved. This will be a haven of healing and equipping as we live on target together.

May we mature in our love for the poor, those in need and the persecuted Church. They all need our support, both in prayer and action.

If we practice these five areas faithfully, we will please our Lord and bless others. We will also position ourselves to be strong disciples and effective disciple-makers. Today, prayerfully make this your aim.

REFLECT AND RESPOND

- How would you describe your love for Christ's Church? What changes are necessary to bring you into a loving relationship with Christ's Church?

- How do you love and serve your local congregation?

- Are there any prejudices or unresolved relationships that you need to address?

- Do you desire to live and worship with all races?

- Are you living community life with other Christians in a small group? Who are you praying for....and who is praying for you?

- How important is communion (The Lord's Supper) to you? Are you participating in communion on a regular basis?

- Is weekly corporate worship part of your lifestyle? Why or why not?

- Do you have compassion for the poor, the persecuted and those who are suffering? How is your concern demonstrated?

Remember, as the Body of Christ, God's reputation is measured by our unity.

SIX

FOUNDATION #4

LIVING IN LOVE AND SERVICE TO THE WORLD

For God so loved the world, that he gave his only begotten Son, that whosoever believeth in him should not perish, but have everlasting life.

– JOHN 3:16 KJV

Thank God He loved us enough to send His Son. But here is a truth we cannot avoid: If God loves the world, then as Christians so should we!

When we mention the word "world" it seems like a very evasive, non-specific place. It almost sounds like too big of a concept. How can we grasp it?

Well, the world starts right where you are, with those who live around you who are not yet Christians.

The book of Acts reminds us that "the world" begins with

the community where you live and then extends outward—until it encompasses the entire planet! *"But you shall receive power when the Holy Spirit has come upon you; and <u>you shall be witnesses to Me</u> in Jerusalem, and in all Judea and Samaria, and to the end of the earth"* (Acts 1:8).

The context here is in the physical nation of Israel with Jerusalem as her capital city. Our "Jerusalem" becomes our own area or town in which we live. As disciples of Christ, pleasing Him includes impacting our communities with the Gospel and with our active presence of love and holiness.

Jesus' command did not say "Jerusalem *or* Judea *or* Samaria *or* the end of the earth." The directive says *"and"* —which means we are to take the message everywhere. As we mature in our discipleship, we will reflect His love for everyone. This is why we need to ask the Lord to give us eyes to view the world the way He does. In this process of Living on Target, loving and serving the *world* will become part of our lifestyle.

THE HARVEST IS READY

Jesus was compassionate toward people who did not know Him. In the Gospel of Matthew we see Him journeying into cities and villages preaching the Gospel and healing people. We read, *"But when He saw the multitudes, <u>He was moved with compassion</u> for them because they were weary and scattered like sheep having no shepherd"* (Matthew 9:36).

Then He said to His disciples, *"The harvest truly is plentiful, but the laborers are few. Therefore pray the Lord of the harvest, to send out laborers into His harvest."* (verses 37-38).

As we are personally making it our aim to be well pleasing to Him, it is essential that we grow in this final foundation. Our Lord is sending us out into the harvest as laborers where we will love lost people—not only in our own local community and country, but be willing to travel (and to send others) to all nations to make disciples for Christ.

It Will Cost Us

If we are honest with ourselves, we all enjoy relaxing, hanging out with our family and friends, having fun and being safe and comfortable. There is nothing inherently wrong with any of these activities, but if they become our life's goals, we will lose the drive to penetrate a lost world and will be ineffective in advancing God's Kingdom.

It will take an intentional effort and it will cost us time, money, reputation, and stepping out of our comfort zones to accomplish the Great Commission and to live out true Christianity. It certainly will take risk, dying to ourselves, and it may even cost us our very lives. *"Then He said to them all, 'If anyone desires to come after Me, let him deny himself, and take up his cross daily, and follow Me'"* (Luke 9:23).

In Philippians 1:20 we read, ..."*according to my earnest expectation and hope that in nothing I shall be ashamed, but with all boldness, as always, so now also Christ will be magnified in my body, whether by life or by death."*

Time is short. Every day people are passing from this life

LIVING ON TARGET

to the next without Christ. Jesus said, *"I must work the works of Him who sent Me while it is day; the night is coming when no one can work"* (John 9:4).

We must fulfill our assignment while we still have time. When we physically die we will then cease from our labors and our deeds will follow us. *"Then I heard a voice from heaven saying to me, 'Write: "Blessed are the dead who die in the Lord from now on." 'Yes,' says the Spirit, "that they may rest from their labors, and their works follow them."* (Revelation 14:13).

May every breath we have and every beat of our heart be used to accomplish our Lord's work. One day we will eternally rest and enjoy the fruit of our labor...but not now! Souls are at stake!

REACHING A LOST WORLD

The Lord gave us a great example of His love for the lost. He was always misunderstood by the Pharisees. These men knew the law of God but sad to say they had forgotten the heart of the Father toward people and had become very "religious." These men were especially perturbed that Jesus would lower Himself to eat with sinners. The true ministry of Jesus still threatens religious people today.

The Bible tells us, *"Now it happened, as Jesus sat at the table in the house, that behold many tax collectors and sinners came and sat down with Him and His disciples. And when the Pharisees saw it, they said to His disciples, 'Why does your Teacher eat with tax collectors and sinners?'"* (Matthew 9:10-11).

176

When Jesus heard their comments, He replied, *"Those that are well have no need of a physician, <u>but those who are sick</u>. But go and learn what this means: 'I desire mercy and not sacrifice.' For I did not come to call the righteous but <u>sinners to repentance</u>"* (verses 12-13).

Jesus was not afraid to associate with sinful people because this was who He came to redeem. These sinners obviously perceived that Jesus was the One who had life because they were drawn to His presence. We need an army of believers who are secure enough in their relationship with Christ to love the way He loves and to penetrate a lost and dying world. We are to call sinners to repentance; not in a haughty and self-righteous manner, but with love and compassion.

NO MORE EXCUSES

Just as Jesus had a heart of mercy for those who were like sheep having no shepherd, we need to ask ourselves, do we carry that same burden and concern? Do we really love those who are lost? Does fear hinder us from evangelizing the lost? In our heart of hearts, would we prefer that someone else reach out to them?

Our neighborhoods and cities are overflowing with people who desperately need Christ. We know this is true, yet we try to justify our apathy, telling ourselves, "Well, I don't want to spend time with this person because they gossip and lie," or "They're selfish," or "They cheat and steal," or "This one does drugs," "This individual is promiscuous...and that one curses"—and the list goes on. *"<u>And such were some of you</u>. But you were washed, but you were sanctified, but you* *were justified in the name of the Lord Jesus and by the Spirit of our God"* (1 Corinthians 6:11). This was our lifestyle before we were saved by the grace of God.

Remember, the same grace that attracted us, continues to draw sinful, broken and hurting people. He loves to take immoral, messy lives and bring His righteousness and order to them. Those who are sinners (as we once were) have uncontrolled lives (like many of ours were).

Sometimes we would prefer not to deal with other people's chaotic conditions or sinful behavior, so we tend to back away instead of pursuing them. They live this way because they are unsaved! We must pursue them with love, acts of kindness, hospitality, and the truth of the Gospel—in word and deed. Their souls are at stake!

We know that we cannot have intimate fellowship with unbelievers because light and darkness have nothing in common (2 Corinthians 6:14). Although we can only have true fellowship with other believers, we can and should pursue nonbelievers with a heart of love and compassion. Let us not become haughty, but convicted to see sinners saved. How much do we really care? Jesus pursued them. So should we!

RESCUED FROM ETERNAL HELL

Do we still believe in hell, and do people still need to be rescued from it? This is not a popular topic today, but none the less one that is a reality.

The Bible is very clear about this horrific place of eternal conscious torment. This fact alone should move us all to conviction and action to see the lost saved.

The reality of a literal place of torment should compel us to witness to everyone at any cost! Please consider our Lord's teaching on this place of anguish:

> There was a certain rich man who was clothed in purple and fine linen and fared sumptuously every day. But there was a certain beggar named Lazarus, full of sores, who was laid at his gate, desiring to be fed with the crumbs which fell from the rich man's table. Moreover the dogs came and licked his sores. So it was that the beggar died, and was carried by the angels to Abraham's bosom. The rich man also died and was buried. _And being in torments in Hades,_ he lifted up his eyes and saw Abraham afar off, and Lazarus in his bosom.
>
> Then he cried and said, "Father Abraham, have mercy on me, and send Lazarus that he may dip the tip of his finger in water and cool my tongue; for _I am tormented in this flame_." But Abraham said, "Son, remember that in your lifetime you received your good things, and likewise Lazarus evil things; but now he is comforted and _you are tormented_. And besides all this, between us and you there is a great gulf fixed, so that those who want to pass from here to you cannot, nor can those from there pass to us."
>
> Then he said, "I beg you therefore, father, that you would send him to my father's house, for I have five brothers, that he may testify to them, lest they also come to this _place of torment_."

Abraham said to him, "They have Moses and the prophets; let them hear them." And he said, "No, father Abraham; but if one goes to them from the dead, they will repent." But he said to him, "If they do not hear Moses and the prophets, neither will they be persuaded though one rise from the dead" (Luke 16:19-31).

Notice that after both men physically died, they were conscious and able to communicate. There absolutely is life after death. The question is where will we spend it—heaven or hell?

Also notice that the word "torment" (in various forms) is used four times in this teaching from Jesus. This fact alone should shake us all to our core! The rich man was in so much anguish that he begged Abraham to send Lazarus back to his father's house so that he could <u>testify</u> to them of this <u>place of torment</u>.

This man wanted his family to repent and not come to this awful destination. If any other person could speak to their family from this literal place they would emphatically say the same thing. We must take hell very seriously and love people enough to warn them. It is literally a matter of life or torment.

Love for a lost world is what moved the Father to send His Son—not to condemn the world but to save it.

Does the truth of an eternal lake of fire compel us to rescue even one soul from this eternal fate? Author John Piper paints a sobering picture of hell in his book, *Let the Nations Be Glad:*

"His winnowing fork is in his hand, and he will clear his threshing floor and gather his wheat into the barn, but the chaff he will burn with unquenchable fire" (Matthew 3:12; Luke 3:17).

This is John the Baptist's prediction of the judgment that Jesus will bring in the end. He pictures a decisive separation. The term *"unquenchable fire"* implies a fire that will not be extinguished and therefore a punishment that will not end. This is confirmed in Mark 9:43-48: *"And if your hand causes you to sin, cut it off. It is better for you to enter life cripple than with two hands to go to hell, to the <u>unquenchable fire</u>. And if your foot causes you to sin, cut it off. It is better for you to enter life lame than with two feet to be thrown into hell. And if your eye causes you to sin, tear it out. It is better for you to enter the kingdom of God with one eye than with two eyes to <u>be thrown into hell, 'where their worm does not die and the fire is not quenched.'"</u>*

Here the *"unquenchable fire"* is clearly hell, and the last line shows that the point is the unending misery of those who go there *("their worm does not die")*.

<u>Hell is a dreadful reality. To speak of it lightly proves that we do not grasp its horror. I know of no one who has overstated the terrors of hell. We can scarcely surpass the horrid images Jesus used. We are meant to shudder.</u>

Here are other scriptures concerning this place of eternal punishment:

- *"And many of those who sleep in the dust of the earth shall awake, some to <u>everlasting life</u>, some to shame and <u>everlasting contempt"</u>* (Daniel 12:2).

- *"And do not fear those who kill the body but cannot kill the soul. But rather fear Him who is able to <u>destroy both soul and body in hell</u>"* (Matthew 10:28).

- *"And these will go away into <u>everlasting punishment</u>, but the righteous into <u>eternal life</u>"* (Matthew 25:46).

- *"[Those] who do not obey the gospel of our Lord Jesus Christ...shall be punished with <u>everlasting destruction</u>"* (2 Thessalonians 1:8-9).

- *"Anyone not found written in the Book of Life was <u>cast into the lake of fire</u>"* (Revelation 20:15).

- *"But the cowardly, unbelieving, abominable, murderers, sexually immoral, sorcerers, idolaters, and all liars <u>shall have their part in the lake which burns with fire and brimstone</u>, which is the second death"* (Revelation 21:8).

I believe these scriptures should shake, convict, and move us all to action. With the reality of hell as a fact, we have a choice to make. With the power of the Holy Spirit we can penetrate a sinful world with the love of Christ and the truth of the Gospel, or...we will excuse ourselves and/or ignore these passages in Scripture.

If we don't stay convicted about the reality of hell, we will attempt to live in a Christian bubble within our own homes and churches and try to stay in a defensive mode. There is certainly nothing wrong with protecting what we believe and why we believe it, however, Jesus has told us to not selfishly keep the Gospel to ourselves, but rather to preach the message to the world. Our Lord is patient toward us, *"...not willing that any should perish but that all should come to repentance"* (2 Peter 3:9).

OUR MANDATE

Jesus declared His followers to be the salt of the earth and the light of the world. *"You are the salt of the earth; but if the salt loses its flavor, how shall it be seasoned? It is then good for nothing but to be thrown out and trampled underfoot by men. You are the light of the world. A city that is set on a hill cannot be hidden"* (Matthew 5:13-14).

The salt and light must not stay within the walls of the church. We are called to evangelize, disciple, and minister, not just where we live, but also globally. We must partner with other Christians around the world to achieve the Great Commission. This mandate is obviously a matter of spiritual life versus eternal damnation. Again, how much do we care?

Jesus said, *"Go therefore and make disciples of all the nations [races], baptizing them in the name of the Father and of the Son and of the Holy Spirit, teaching them to observe all things that I have commanded you; and lo, I am with you always, even to the end of the age"* (Matthew 28:19-20).

This mission has been given to all of us, not just specific

183

leaders in the church. The enemy will tell you that you are not qualified. A Bible degree, though very valuable, is not a requirement for witnessing to the lost or discipling the saved. When we share our testimony of salvation and the Gospel message of repentance and faith in Christ alone, the Holy Spirit will accomplish His work.

We do not have the power to save anyone. The Holy Spirit convicts of sin and God the Father draws a person to salvation. Our role is simply to love and testify that Jesus Christ is the only way to the Father and salvation. *"Jesus said to him, "I am the way, the truth, and the life. <u>No one comes to the Father except through Me</u>"* (John 14:6).

As we share the Gospel and people repent and come to faith in Christ, we now have the privilege of welcoming them to the family of God and asking if they would allow us to show them how we live our lives aiming to be pleasing to the Lord.

The moment they receive Christ we have the privilege of asking if we may disciple them. It naturally flows out of our walk with Him and into our life with the new disciple. It is not a program or a rigid religious schedule. If we have been discipled, then we continue the legacy. If we were not discipled early on, we can begin the legacy.

Some of the greatest witnesses in the church today are individuals who were just recently saved. They have a zeal and passion to tell others what the Lord has just accomplished in their lives. This process of discipleship is not nearly as intimidating as others have made it to be. *It is simply teaching and modeling for somebody else what you are already doing...thus the importance of Living on Target.*

In order for the majority of the church to live in love and

service to the world (Foundation Four) we must be living faithfully in the first three foundations. Then we will have the time, availability, integrity, and passion for missions. The "charge" for the church is to make disciples of all nations. Since God is a missionary God and He desires for all people to come to repentance, then missions should be a priority for His church. This includes <u>every</u> Christian. He calls us <u>all</u> to participate.

A HEART TO REACH THE WORLD

The Lord has called each and every one of us to be witnesses for Him through the power of the Holy Spirit. If we want the church to be strong in missions, then it is imperative that we have the other foundations in order so that the Great Commission can become a primary emphasis in our personal life as well.

Fulfilling the Great Commission doesn't mean that each of us will sell all we own and move to another country. While some will be called to such a ministry, we are all commissioned to participate through prayer, through our own active service of sharing the Gospel wherever we live, through our giving, and staying united in the Great Commission until every man, woman, and child has heard the Gospel of Jesus.

I earnestly pray this mission stirs your heart to the point that evangelism and discipleship become an integral part of your life. This is an eternal goal and a biblical aim. This is Living on Target!

REFLECT AND RESPOND

- Have you counted the cost of true Christianity? In light of that, are you willing to live for, and be persecuted for Christ?

- What conclusions have you come to about the place of torment and do you believe that people need to be rescued from it?

- What are you doing to own the "lostness" of your neighbors, your city, and the world? What could be more important than saving a soul from hell?

- What do you think it means to be salt and light?

- Do you love unbelievers? If so, how do you share your faith with them?

- How are you participating in the Great Commission?

Remember, with God nothing is impossible!

SEVEN

THE PROCESS OF DISCIPLESHIP

Therefore go and make disciples of all nations, baptizing them in the name of the Father and of the Son and of the Holy Spirit, and teaching them to obey everything I have commanded you. And surely I am with you always, to the very end of the age.

— MATTHEW 28:19

The four foundations of Living on Target are not only for your personal spiritual growth, they are designed to equip you to invest your life in others. Yes, to make disciples. How can we make this happen?

We must live what we believe and teach. We are not perfect, but if we are faithful in Living on Target, we can simply (with humility) encourage others to follow our example. This is a goal every Christian should aim for.

Safe Environments

One of the foremost aspects of becoming an effective discipler is to learn to listen far more than we speak. James 1:19 tells us, *"So then, my beloved brethren, let every man be <u>swift to hear</u>, <u>slow to speak</u>, slow to wrath;"* This includes having ears to hear what the Spirit has to say and what the person we're discipling has to say. People will not care how much of the Bible we know until they understand that we truly care about them. We must learn how to be good listeners—<u>then</u> speak words of life into them.

We need to be pro-active in creating safe environments in our churches where people can confess their sins and struggles without feeling judged, condemned, or looked down upon. James 5:16 says, *"Confess your trespasses to one another, and pray for one another, that you may be healed. The effective, fervent prayer of a righteous man avails much."*

Could it be that we have stopped confessing sin to one another in the church because of our gossiping? Could we experience more healings if we started confessing sins and praying for one another in gossip-free environments where mercy and grace are found? This was certainly the ministry of Jesus when the Scribes and Pharisees brought the woman caught in adultery to Him to have her stoned to death (John 8:1-11).

They demanded her stoning because of the letter of the law. Yet Jesus, who embodied righteousness, extended mercy and life. He saw her brokenness and responded with compassion. The religious leaders dropped their stones because they knew that they all had sinned and fallen short of the glory of God.

Jesus was not soft on sin. Rather, He was strong in mercy. Like a father to a daughter, Jesus told this woman that He did not condemn her but now she should go "and sin no more."

I want to meet this woman in heaven, don't you? I wish we had a record of her life—after her encounter with Jesus. Can you imagine her gratefulness knowing that she should have died, but that Jesus extended mercy and life?

The reality is that we <u>are</u> her! We have all fallen short of His glory. Each of us stands before God having broken His righteous law. We all deserve death and torment. But praise God, we have been extended mercy and forgiveness, just as she was! We can all be thankful for His saving grace.

Do we minister like the religious people, stones in our hands, ready to condemn? Or, like Jesus, are we willing to extend compassion and mercy when we encounter broken lives and hearts?

The Church of Jesus Christ must minister like Him, breathing life into people instead of condemnation. If we don't minister in the manner of our Lord, we should not call ourselves a church—but rather, an institution dispensing Bible knowledge with no heart or life changing power. Hypocrites honor Him with their lips but their hearts are far from Him (Mark 7:6-8). Where is your heart?

The Apostle Paul did not just teach and preach, but he invested his life into people—and loved those he discipled. To the believers at Thessalonica, he wrote, *"But we were gentle among you, just as a nursing mother cherishes her own children. So, affectionately longing for you, we were*

well pleased to impart to you not only the gospel of God,
<u>*but also our own lives, because you had become dear to us*</u>
(1 Thessalonians 2:7-8).

What a marvelous example. Paul wasn't just an apostle or a gifted teacher, he wanted to live life with those he deeply cared for. Let us follow his example.

SHARE YOUR STORY

To initiate the discipling process, start by getting to know the person. Sit down over a cup of coffee and share your life stories. Since most people are reluctant to open up to someone they don't know, feel free to tell a little about your life first. But keep it short. Then, at the appropriate moment, ask, "Would you mind sharing your story with me?"

I led my first Living on Target group with the other pastors on my staff. Even though some of us had been laboring together in the church for several years, we had not taken the time to share our life stories as a group.

We listened and learned a lot about each other. We confessed our struggles, gave words of encouragement, and prayed together. This investment of our time deepened our trust and appreciation for each other tremendously—and this process cannot be bypassed with anyone we disciple. This principle applies to people you have known for years and to those you are just meeting.

Such an exchange is necessary since you need to know a person's heart—and they need to know yours. Your early meetings should center on developing trust, offering encouragement and prayer.

As trust develops, more intimate issues may be shared. Keep conversations very confidential. Continue to breathe life into that individual, laying the groundwork for the further discipling that will take place as your relationship deepens.

DISCIPLING IN REAL LIFE

Let me share this account of how this process unfolds in real life:

A gentleman came to our church one Sunday and sat on the back row. The message touched him and he came forward at the end of the service. He was broken before God and desperate to change.

This man was an alcoholic with a tragic story. He had grown up in an alcoholic family where his father was abusive and regularly told him. "You'll never amount to anything." Weeks prior to God touching him, his mother had died in his arms after an accident, his brother had committed suicide, he had been abusive to his wife, was about to lose his marriage, and was contemplating suicide.

As he came to the front for prayer, one of our leaders was able to connect him with a discipler who met with him weekly to <u>listen</u> and <u>pray</u>. This went on for several months. Then he got connected to a home fellowship group to participate with the men in a bi-weekly Living on Target discipleship meeting. Through this process, the man has been able to hear directly from God through the Holy Spirit about who the Lord says he is—rather than allowing his actions or others to *define him. He now accepts that he has great value to God and that the Lord has uniquely gifted him for a purpose. His life now has hope.*

He has learned how to walk with God through regular reading of the Bible, prayer, and worship. Another gentleman from the group has taken ownership of walking along side of him to teach him how to manage his finances as a steward of God.

It's now been nearly two years since he originally walked into the church. He's certainly not perfect, but he is on the right path.

The discipler just reported receiving a call from him saying, "I have another friend who needs help. I want to disciple him like you are discipling me!"

It's amazing how the discipling process works in real life with real people. We have a real God! May this process of making disciples continue for His glory and the expansion of His Kingdom.

LIVING THE FOUR FOUNDATIONS

Begin sharing with the person you are discipling about how you are practicing the spiritual disciplines of Living on Target. Talk about the victories you have had in the past week in these areas, such as specific answers to prayer, advances you have made in your role as a husband or wife, someone you shared the Gospel with, a person you served in need, etc.

Be honest about your challenges as well—when you were

humbled, or just blew it! "I haven't had a quiet time in the last four days," or "I missed my son's ball game because I was working too much," or "I mistreated my spouse and yelled at my children," or "I missed communion last weekend because I was in a bad mood," etc.

Transparency and confession makes way for the people we disciple to be open and transparent. We have a spiritual objective that we're aiming for, but we all realize that at times, we fall short. It gives us opportunity to celebrate when we are being faithful and to pray for each other to become faithful when we haven't been. This is why we have constantly stated in this book that Living on Target is a lifestyle.

We should continue to grow in all of these areas as we press forward to become all that Christ has intended us to be. There is always room to grow and mature—thus the need for discipleship based on a spiritual target:

1. **Living in Love and Service to Christ**
   Becoming men and women of *prayer*, the *Word*, and *personal worship*.

2. **Living in Love and Service in the Home**
   Placing our homes, singleness, marriages, children, and finances in biblical order.

3. **Living in Love and Service to the Church**
   Loving the Bride of Christ and being united in purpose. Ministering to the poor, the persecuted and those in need.

4. **Living in Love and Service to the World**
   Loving and pursuing the lost. Evangelizing and discipling. Giving a clear, authentic witness for Christ and His salvation.

PREACH JESUS, WARN AND TEACH

Paul was forthright regarding exactly *how* to accomplish the discipling process. He preached Jesus! *"Him we preach, warning every man and teaching every man in all wisdom, that we may present every man [every person] perfect [or mature] in Christ Jesus"* (Colossians 1: 28).

We should not be talking about some generic God, but rather, boldly proclaiming Jesus as the Way, the Truth, and the Life (John 14:6). We are not to be timid or afraid to warn those we love. We are to tell them:

- Jesus is the only way to the Father.
- There is a real heaven and a real hell.
- There are consequences to sin, but there is power to live a godly life.

Paul did not compromise on the authority and divinity of Jesus, and he also warned people of the results of sin. He taught and modeled for them how to live a life that is pleasing to God. So should we.

A LABOR OF LOVE

What a privilege we have to equip others to become

disciples—leading them to walk in the identity they have in Christ and experience the purpose He has for them.

Please understand, discipling is not just going to happen because of desire. There is hard work involved. As Paul states, *"To this end I also labor, striving according to His working which works in me mightily"* (Colossians 1:29).

The good news is that God does the work through us. He is the One who actually accomplishes the discipling. The Lord is simply looking for vessels who are willing to be used for His glory.

People will not mature as fast as we would like them to, but don't ever give up on them—especially since Christ did not give up on us! Paul expressed disappointment in people but he labored with them until he saw Christ fully formed in their lives (Galatians 4:19). Let us follow His example and labor of love with others for the sake of their maturity in Christ. Great will be our reward. May they become our joy and crown (Philippians 4:1; 1 Thessalonians 2:19).

How Will You Live?

The instruction, warning, and encouragement have been given. It *does* matter how we live on this earth. We will stand at the Judgment Seat of Christ and will give an account of our love, devotion, work, and motives. Unbelievers will also face judgment and will be sentenced and cast into the Lake of Fire.

To the unbeliever, or seeker, according to John 14:6 and Acts 4:10, Jesus is the only way to the Father. I pray you will repent, surrender, and give your life to Jesus today. Find a

Bible-believing and teaching church where people will not only instruct you in the Gospel, but will invest their lives into you personally and relationally. Every Christian needs to live in community with other believers, to have a safe place where honesty, transparency, confession, and learning can occur without condemnation.

I am an optimistic person—and I feel this way toward the Church. I believe the Body of Christ is the greatest organism in the world and I am honored to be part of Her and even to help lead Her in some small way. I pray the Lord will unite us together to have the impact in these last days that is needed on behalf of a lost and dying humanity.

QUESTIONS WE MUST ANSWER

The reason I have written this book is to encourage us to get back to the original plan the Lord gave us to change the world: "GO MAKE DISCIPLES!"

But let's be honest. How many disciples have we personally made in the last year—two—three—how about ten years? We must ask ourselves the question, "Why are we not effective in discipling?"

Today, we can get more caught up in just "going" to church, while we miss the reality of "being" the Church. Our presence at a Sunday service or a Bible study is certainly important, and many of us are there regularly—and should be. But why don't we see more life changes, more love, peace, joy and contentment, more passion for Christ, for our spouses, and intentional parenting of our children? Why don't we find more generous giving or more disciple makers and servants in the Church? Where is that unwavering commitment to fulfill the Great Commission in Jesus' name?

The Church will not have the power or impact that She could have until every member first learns how to commune with God by themselves in the quiet place and stay empowered by the Holy Spirit. This is where our hearts are constantly spoken to, healed, encouraged, convicted, corrected, and empowered by the Lord. It is here where sons and daughters of God begin to function as they were designed, where marriages are restored, where parents and children are convicted and given new life, where God's money is released back into His hands, where the Church is loved, discipled, and prayed for, and where the persecuted, poor and lost become a passion for us.

ONLY BY GOD'S SPIRIT

Over two thousand years ago, Paul wrote a letter to the church at Galatia. They started their Christian walk in the Spirit, yet, over time, they tried to perfect themselves by means of their flesh.

As I read church history and observe the challenges of the modern church, it seems very clear to me that the same temptation is with us today. Even with our best intentions, it appears we all face the temptation to perfect ourselves by our own logic, reasoning, and personal attempts at good behavior.

Every leader desires to find the keys to leading a fruitful church. We are in a constant search for the right curriculum, the right program, the right strategy or method. In order to grow the church and to heal and mature people in the faith, we seem to run to other individuals or programs looking for the "silver bullet."

In reality, no human being or human program can transform a person's heart. We have been attempting to change people in the flesh for far too long. In the process, we have become frustrated, disappointed, or worn out trying to "fix" people. We do not have the ability to repair lives, but we have been empowered to lead men and women to the One who can!

If we would teach and model how to experience the presence of God and the power of the Holy Spirit on a daily basis, we should certainly see ongoing transformation in lives.

<u>We cannot substitute His divine presence for anything—even good things. He is our ultimate source and life changer! Lead people to meet Him in the quiet place.</u>

START LIVING ON TARGET TODAY

Let me emphasize again that I believe the greatest tool we can give to ourselves and others to mature in our faith is the quiet place—the haven where we develop ears to hear what the Spirit has to say to us.

Our flesh, Satan, and our busyness will fight against solitude and being still long enough to commune with God. When we discover and abide habitually in the quiet place with the Almighty, revival and a fruitful life will be ours.

Our primary ministry as a Christian is to minister first and foremost unto our Lord. Our labor for God will come from our love for Him and from our time spent with Him.

There is a price to be paid for living a life well pleasing unto God, yet that has always been the call of Christianity.

Jesus is still saying: *"If anyone desires to come after Me, let him deny himself, and take up his cross daily, and follow Me. For whoever desires to save his life will lose it, but whoever loses his life for My sake will save it. For what profit is it to a man if he gains the whole world, and is himself destroyed or lost? For whoever is ashamed of Me and My words, of him the Son of Man will be ashamed when He comes in His own glory, and in His Father's, and of the holy angels"* (Luke 9:23-26). Stand firm in Christ!

A life lived by denying self and taking up one's cross daily and following Him brings joy, contentment, purpose, hope, and the abundant life. We must abandon cultural Christianity and fully embrace biblical Christianity in order to please our Lord. May we all aim at Living on Target each day in honor of Christ as we eagerly await His return. To Him and Him along be all glory, praise, and honor!

REFLECT AND RESPOND

- In what ways have you spiritually invested yourself in the lives of others? Do you consider yourself a "safe person" to whom others can come to be discipled?

- Are you willing to proclaim Christ—warning and teaching (in word and lifestyle) so that others may mature in Christ?

- Are you willing to accept that the discipling process is costly in time, resources, and labor (but worth every minute)?

- Do you see the importance of Living on Target as a lifestyle until Jesus comes for us?

- Evaluate the four foundations of Living on Target as they relate to you. In which are you the strongest? Where do you need to develop and mature?

- What changes are you committed to make as a result of reading this book?

Maranatha—Our Lord Come Quickly!

THE IMPACT OF LIVING ON TARGET

Space does not permit me to share the countless stories of men and women who have been touched by being discipled in Living on Target.

Here are the personal accounts of four individuals whose lives have been changed:

From a mom:

I used to be so busy with work, being a mom and wife and working in church activities. I kept my inner life hidden. I wore the mask of perfection well and stayed in my dark place of struggles for a very long time.

To talk to anyone else about my inner battles seemed unfamiliar and wrong. "People are looking up to you. Never let them see you sweat, hurt or cry." Mentally, that kept me in bondage until three years ago.

I began a relationship with a Living on Target group. God used this to change my life! I was becoming accountable and transparent. My relationships have been different. First my relationship with the Lord became personal and alive. Satan could no longer hold my past over me—causing me to think that I was unworthy to serve.

There was freedom in being transparent with others whom the Lord placed in my life for that purpose. To have people know my true struggles in life and have them walk alongside of me, praying for me, holding me accountable in life because they loved me was wonderful. That they cared and desired to see me grow was—and still is—amazing!

I have learned that Living on Target is not simply something you do once and then it's over. It is not something you 'go through' and you're done. It is a lifestyle. It is a daily walk with the One who pursues and desires to be in relationship with you. It is a lifestyle to be modeled in any setting to bring individuals into a real love relationship with Jesus Christ, others, the church, and the world!

From a dad:

The Living on Target discipleship model has been life changing for me as well as my family. The simplistic focus on four areas: Love and Service to Christ, Home, Church, and the World has shaped and continues to shape how we structure our day-to-day lives into a Christ passion-driven life.

Recognizing that Living on Target is a lifestyle and not just a discipleship tool has been liberating. At the core of all our decisions as a family is this question: With the time we have in each day, how can we continue to focus on developing a more meaningful and intimate relationship with Jesus Christ—with my wife as well as her relationship with me, our relationship with our children as well as with our extended family?

In our love and service to the church and the world, we pose the same question. With the giftings, resources, and ministries the Holy Spirit has empowered us with as a family, how can they be used to further develop meaningful relationships with our Christian family and those who do not know Christ? The focus of meaningful relationships is defined in the areas (we call the "ships"): Worship, Fellowship, Discipleship, and Friendship.

Finally, one is always processing 2 Timothy 2:2 in relation to each of the four areas as a discipler. How can I develop meaningful relationships within my family and the Body of Christ in order to disciple them in a way they can disciple others?

In other words, to disciple in a way to accomplish Matthew 28:20 within each life God has ordained you to touch—so they, too, will be able to observe all that God has commanded.

From a young woman:

It is nearly impossible to put into words how Living on Target has affected my life. I was only a junior in high school when I went through the process with my small group, and I can say beyond a shadow of a doubt that my life has been radically changed by something incredibly simple.

I have had my fair share of useful and enlightening Bible studies, but nothing compares to what Living on Target offers a person when it is modeled accurately.

203

Living on Target is something which changes a person's life from the inside out, gives a person a biblical foundation to stand on and shows him how to live a life that is pleasing to the Lord. And this is exactly what it has done in me through the power of the Holy Spirit. It has taken me to a place of absolute intimacy in my relationship with the Lord, a place I had never before experienced, and a place that keeps me hungry and thirsty for more of Jesus every day.

My quiet times—even the notion of that was new to me when I started Living on Target—have become my daily source of life, strength, joy, and excitement. The list goes on and on, because when I meet with Him I encounter a perfect God who loves me even in my imperfection and I discover that He is my everything and I am in such desperate need of Him.

I am humbled by my Heavenly Father like a little girl is when she gets to spend that privileged alone time with her papa and knows that she is dearly and affectionately loved. I have come to realize just how protective I am of that alone time I spend with Him; for when I make God the very center of my life and allow Him to pour into me, every other aspect of life is affected by it as well, and a steady reflection of Christ begins to shine through. I cannot stand in the presence of God and not be changed.

Living on Target, and the woman who mentored me along the way, has led me to the feet of Jesus and He has captured my heart. It is something which constantly takes me to a deeper place in my faith and draws me closer to Him in my walk.

From a discipler:

An attractive young lady in her twenties was hurt, and emotionally wounded. She was unsure about God and even though she grew up in a Christian home, she had never fully received a relationship with Christ as her own, but she wasn't aware of this at the time. She was seeking something in the world to validate her existence. She turned to cutting herself, bulimia, alcohol and drugs. She was trying to numb herself from the pains of life.

When she came to the church, a couple of women took time to meet with her, to listen to her story and pray for her. She appreciated their time, but she wasn't yet ready to accept the truth.

She left and we didn't see her for a while. Then one of the ladies who had prayed with her got a call from the young lady's parents saying that she had tried to commit suicide and she was refusing to speak with anyone but this woman who had prayed for her. They had a chance to meet and talk again.

The woman encouraged her and shared that she really could have her own relationship with God, that He loved her and wanted to spend time with her. They continued to meet and the young lady entered a Christian recovery program. The woman faithfully drove her to the program which was several hours away.

She would go to visit her to encourage her. She wrote letters, and provided a room in her house when the young lady graduated from the program, so she could adjust and transition back into the work world. She regularly prayed for her.

The young lady received a real relationship with Christ where she can pray to Him and He speaks to her. He loves her and she knows it.

The young lady is now active in the church and a part of a Living on Target discipling group. She is learning how to live a Christian life and get her finances in order. She works at a local ministry and desires to learn how to listen to and pray for others who are hurting. Her future has purpose and she enjoys all of the feelings and emotions of life, desiring others to experience what she has in Christ.

A FINAL WORD

Let me encourage you to take the principles found on these pages and begin Living on Target as your lifestyle.

I am praying that the Lord will use this to help form your spiritual development—and those with whom you come in contact—to continue in the faith, become grounded and steadfast in Him until His return (Colossians 1:21-23).

If Living on Target has made an impact on your life or your church, we would love to hear your story.

May God richly bless you and use you for His glory!

– Kelvin Smith

For Additional information about
Living on Target
Contact

Living on Target
Steele Creek Church of Charlotte
1929 West Arrowood Road
Charlotte, NC 28217

Phone: 704-525-1133
Internet: www.livingontarget.org
www.steelecreek.org